This book is dedicated to the divine creative spark

lying at the heart of each and everyone of us

Visions of Reality

Barbara Rose

Art of Synthesis

AuthorHouse™ UK Ltd.
500 Avebury Boulevard
Central Milton Keynes, MK9 2BE
www.authorhouse.co.uk
Phone: 08001974150

First published by AuthorHouse 4/23/2010

ISBN: 978-1-4490-6650-5 (sc)

Galactic content within images: NASA/courtesy of nasaimages.org.
Cover design: Barbara Rose

This book is printed on acid-free paper.

authorHOUSE®

Table of Contents

Tables and Illustrations

Foreword by Angela Morse

Many traditions and teachings speak to us about the divine essence that is within each of us. In the past that knowledge has been spoken of quietly, to a select few, or written of in arcane language. That secretiveness is no longer appropriate. It is now time for us all to share in the knowledge of whom and what we are. How do we find that essence within us? How do we know when we have found it? These important questions have many answers, only some will be relevant to each individual person. It is helpful to acknowledge that the quest can be difficult. There is no map to guide us, no instructions to tell us how to journey. However there is a theme we can discern from the experiences and shared stories of those who have gone before us. The prime methods are through sound and imaging. Sound includes song, dance, sacred chant, drumming, music and poetry. These all rely heavily upon, and invoke our feeling nature. Visual imaging too, primarily uses feeling, creating visual landscapes that express our inner world. Whilst our mind and our intellect may play a role in understanding and interpreting, it is a minor role, and is not leading the experience.

The demands of a busy daily life mean that we all too often live our life at the outer edges of who we are. Led by the stresses of all those "essential" chores, we employ our mind almost exclusively in its thinking, analytical and logical mode (the beta state) and we rarely have time to contemplate the richness of our inner world. We soon forget how to. We are no longer whole, no longer aware of our inner sacredness, the true wellspring of our being. When we employ a contemplative feeling mode, whether we realise it or not, we more easily access that inner world. This can connect us to our inner joy, our peace, and our strengths. Our inner light sustains and nourishes our life at all levels and we flourish. However, within our inner world, we may also encounter our shadow side, which is just as valid and real. Here we find our "emotional clutter"; our inner resentments, our pain from rejection or abandonment, our feeling of being let down or not valued. We may recoil. We do not relish experiencing again those negative emotions. It might help us to realise those negative feelings are just energetic remembrance forms, creating layers over our inner sacred core. When they do they hide or mask our brilliance. Fortunately for us, if we can learn to trust our inner innate wisd transmute and release those layers of emotional residue. When we bring them into the focus and see them for what they are, they no longer have power over us. Identification with us to ponder, to reflect, and to make new choices that lead us back to wholeness and peace. We become the Inner Alchemist, taking the dross of gross emotion and transforming it into golden light illuminating the divine spark at the core of our being.

Personal and spiritual development is like a journey along a spiral winding its way upward and onward towards wholeness. Wherever you are on this spiral, this book can help you on your journey. One of the strengths of this work is that it draws on the wisdom and insights of several traditions. However there is no need to study or understand these traditions in order to work with the images, poetry and seed thoughts. It follows therefore that no-one is telling you what to do or how to be. I think this is such an important gift. We are being encouraged to explore our inner world in a way that allows our own intuition and our own authentic responses to guide us. We go as far as we wish, and at whatever pace we choose. The inner process of growth and change has its own natural timing and this book both respects and encourages that.

These images are Barbara's. So too are the poems and seed thoughts. Your responses, the welling up of feelings, are solely your own. Some images or poems will move you more than others, and you will respond differently at different times. Notice that. As one poem moved me to tears, I resonated with the feeling behind the words. I knew that here was an issue to stay with for a while, to reflect on, to hold in my consciousness. Holding the feeling allowed my deep inner sacred core to bathe me in its love and communicate "all is well, you are not alone, you never were and never will be." This kind of inner message needs to be held for some time to allow it to permeate through every fibre of our being until we have no doubt whatsoever that it is our Truth. We come out of that process changed, stronger, healed and more whole.

It is rare to find a book of this genre that can be worked with wherever you are on your spiral of development. It is rare too, to find a book of wisdom that so generously empowers you to see your own inner sacredness. However you use this book, know that it is both Transpersonal and Alchemical. It really does what it says on the cover, it is the "Art of Synthesis".

Angela Morse
Durham
December 2009

The Great Invocation

From the point of light within the mind of God
Let light stream forth into human minds
Let light descend on earth
From the point of love within the heart of God
Let love pour forth into human hearts
May the coming One return to earth
From the centre where the will of God is known
Let purpose guide all little human wills
The purpose which the masters know and serve
From the centre which we call the human race
Let the plan of love and light work out
And may it seal the door where evil dwells
Let light and love and power
Restore the plan on earth

"*The above Invocation or Prayer does not belong to any person or group but to all Humanity. The beauty and the strength of this Invocation lies in its simplicity, and in its expression of certain central truths which all men, innately and normally, accept—the truth of the existence of a basic Intelligence to Whom we vaguely give the name of God; the truth that behind all outer seeming, the motivating power of the universe is Love; the truth that a great Individuality came to earth, called by Christians, the Christ, and embodied that love so that we could understand; the truth that both love and intelligence are effects of what is called the Will of God; and finally the self-evident truth that only through humanity itself can the Divine Plan work out.*"

ALICE A. BAILEY

Introduction

...from within the Great Void

A sound is heard...

Vibration Pure Light

Travels to the heart of existence...

Light of Truth... Light of Love... Light of Power...

As fractals of rainbow light

Become aspects of reality

Truth appears in myriad form

The Way is shown...

The time is NOW...

The message is clear...

BE WHO YOU ARE!

"Manifest the beauty of your Soul...

walk a rainbow through your life..."

Welcome to Visions of Reality...

an invitation for you to embark upon a life-long journey of self discovery. The preceding script holds the essence of this creative work and illustrates the purpose for which it was born. A bridge between levels of existence, it serves as a reminder and guide for us to walk upon this earth in full remembrance of who we really are: multi-dimensional beings of light reflecting All That Is.

Every living being is born to a purpose and, in the case of a human being, if that purpose becomes known, life ceases to be a struggle. 'Visions of Reality' *art of synthesis* offers the opportunity for you to experience the highest aspect of your being. When you achieve this, your purpose becomes more readily accessible leading to inner joy and natural abundance in your daily life.

Many traditions - east and west, ancient and modern - come together for those who seek understanding and inner knowing of these most profound teachings. Simple contemplation of drawings, seed thoughts and poems offer opportunity for the light of Truth to awaken from within, facilitating the transition from separation to unity consciousness. No matter where you are on your journey, if you are drawn to this work, it will serve to inspire and uplift assisting you in your daily life during these times of monumental change.

Namaste...

Appreciation

As I reflect upon the 'Visions' journey and warm to the many varied sources that have inspired and contributed to its final perfected form, I realise it to be a product of group consciousness.

Family and friends, animal and cetacean, teachers and students, the wind and the rain, earth and the stars; some seen, some intangible, some known whilst others strangers; even the betrayers have played their part.

To set aside any one of these as expression of gratitude would be to dishonour the rest. What right do I have to make a particle of that which is, in Truth, a wave? How can I make separate that which is already whole? Some are mentioned within the pages of this book some are not but are they any less worthy of appreciation?

In keeping with the true spirit of Visions of Reality there is only one thing left to be said...

Thank you One, and all

A Story of Creation

The origin, the point of light, from which all structures are made manifest, according to ancient kabbalistic tradition, follows a natural and divine order.

In the highest level of existence God, the Creator, abides as limitless pure light; a state of negative existence known as 'Ain Sof' (meaning without end).

The first act of creation found Ain Sof contracting into itself to create a space from which the finite world may be made manifest, a void of emptiness being left in its stead. Without this contraction there would not have been space for creation to materialise as all was limitless light.

Into the space thus created Ain Sof sent forth a beam of light that became the first of four kabbalistic worlds; each subsequent emanation being a step down in vibration with the last, the world of matter, being the most dense. The ten spheres of the Tree of Life, along with the 22 linking paths, play essential parts in the evolution of this process.

In summary: for creation to occur there must be contraction, a concentration of energy to a single point followed by an expansion, an emanation into the space thus created.

This continuous process of contraction and expansion sets the scene for every creative process throughout all levels of existence. It runs as a river through the pages of this book and is a wise practise to adopt during contemplation of the material contained therein. The same process may also be applied when using the visions as tools to enhance everyday life.

Contraction may be seen as turning within, withdrawal of energy from any external distraction, including thought processes and emotional responses. This contraction creates a space, referred to as void in the story above, where all is still. It is the pause between thought, between words, between each breath and each heartbeat; a pause that is pregnant with infinite possibilities. It is this space, the pause which generates expansion quite spontaneously.

Contraction and expansion follow natural order during contemplation but is less difficult to apply in daily life; however the principle remains the same no matter what the outer circumstances. Return to the breath. Simply breathe. Place your attention on the pause between each in and each out breath and it will always bring you back to the pregnant pause, the creative space that delivers respons-*ability*; action not reaction. At the heart of this process lies a constant attitude of surrender with every let-go seeing a deepening into and subsequent expansion of the void. This is soul integration.

Visions of Reality - the journey

The 'Visions' journey began in the summer of 2005 following a retreat at Samye Ling Buddhist monastery in Scotland. I re-connected with an 'old' friend who stirred memories of times we had shared in service spanning many aeons of time. I believe her to be a channel for immense creative energy and somehow an aspect of this awakened during our first moments of re-connection.

On my return from Scotland I set about completing a personal development exercise we were given during the retreat. The remit was to create a drawing containing a tree, a river, a house, a sun and a snake; each of them representing 'role models' in early life. Even in Scotland I had an idea as to how this drawing would appear but the surprise came when I believed I had finished.

Having included all the required elements, I began shading in the background... I just wanted to fill it with soft, golden light. I continued 'doodling' for what seemed like hours until I felt it was done. When I stepped back to view the drawing, I could not believe what lay before my eyes... a beautiful, golden being emanating purity, gentleness and love was gazing back at me. I wept at the wonder of this beautiful creation. "My God what have I drawn?" were the only words I could find as I continued to stand transfixed upon the most benevolent being I had ever laid eyes upon. I named it 'Emergence' for it seemed the being literally emerged as I was doodling.

The second drawing 'Recognition' appeared a few days later as an offering and in remembrance of my old friend who had sparked this re-emergence of creativity. The seed thought also reflects this encounter and begins with her initial greeting on that most auspicious of days: "Hello, Little Brother".

One by one the drawings appeared inspired either through meditation or through events unfolding in my daily life. 'Beings' would appear as I became more relaxed and 'played' with the different colours and shadings. I was in absolute awe over the whole process for I, literally, did not believe I had it in me!

With the unfolding of each creation I soon came to realise aspects of self being revealed. I became more complete, more whole and more aware as a result. Each drawing, poem and seed thought has been a joy to create and has appeared in its own time with seemingly minimal effort. Certainly in the early days I had no predetermined goals, I simply drew and wrote for the pure joy of creating. They evolved initially as a pack of contemplation cards later materialising into its current form.

The 'golden beings' became the 'golden age' and eventually, some three years later, evolved into the 'Love' set. They represent an era where peace, harmony, joy, fun and ancient wisdom were foundations for life. The drawings stirred memories and feelings of times spent in ancient Atlantis and, particularly for me, ancient Lemuria. I believe with each emerging presence another aspect was, quite literally, being born into light.

During 2006 I began exploring another medium of creative expression: computer graphics and image manipulation. I had dabbled with this medium for many years; it was play and fun time during my days off from work. I started viewing images I had previously created – fantasy art, photographic collages, cats and dogs in space etc – in particular I wanted to see the 'layers' that contributed to the finished article.

Several levels beneath the surface of one of them was the drawing 'Unicorn'. Now unicorns are connected to the 5th or 7th dimension (depending on sources), and are said to represent the ascended master of the horse. As such they hold a very pure vibration and light. This picture had been hanging on my wall for almost ten years as one of the layers hidden beneath a 'Dog's View of Heaven' collage. I had been totally unaware of its presence yet it was a picture I never replaced. It hangs on my wall in its original 'doggie' form even now. So much for my believing I never had it in me. The evidence hangs right before my eyes to this day!

By the end of 2006 I had completed some twenty drawings. Feedback from friends suggested they could be made into a set of cards so I began to add short verses of prose as a further aid to contemplation. The first of these was 'Phone Home'. It came at a time when I was increasingly aware of my alien heritage yet feeling very much alone and isolated in that knowing. The drawing itself filled me with encouragement and love for it showed, far from being isolated on a strange planet, I was surrounded by brothers and sisters from distant galaxies. I simply had to open my eyes and expand my heart in order to welcome them into my life.

Unification occurred within as I realised aspects in their entirety; human, alien, galaxy and earth were simply reflections of one unified consciousness. The poem expands upon these sentiments and serves as a reminder for each one of us to embrace all these parts as features of our true nature. The title came as I contemplated the 'being' on the right side of the picture; he seemed to be so much a part of this earth with no separation between him and the land. He was of the earth and yet in communion with alien beings. He reminded me of 'ET' so 'Phone Home' became the obvious title.

At this time I joined a weekly meditation group to explore the pathways of the Kabbalah. I had been interested in these teachings since my teenage years and had studied them somewhat sporadically for more than thirty years. The meditations led to deeper understanding and I began to see a connection between the teachings of the Kabbalah and the 'Visions' project. My insight was to produce 33 cards, one for each of eleven 'Sephira' (spheres) and one for each of the 22 linking paths. This structure is known as the 'Tree of Life' and holds within it many secrets for man's evolution to spirit and spirit's involution into matter. The drawing 'Becoming' contains this structure with the seed thought and poem being means for contemplating this work further. The Kabbalah also links to the seven chakra system found in many eastern spiritual traditions. The idea of contemplation cards linking ancient traditions and teachings within one medium was born.

Having shared my idea with a small group, my ancient friend suggested there should be 33 + 1 cards; the +1 being the one that transcended all the systems. This suggestion sent shivers down my spine and became a part of the 'Vision'. The work was evolving and expanding already and once again it was with minimal effort.

In the spring of 2006, following a series of quite remarkable co-incidences, I stumbled across sacred geometry. I went to the yoga show (not an event I would normally be drawn to) in Manchester for a spontaneous afternoon out with a friend. As soon as we walked in, we were greeted by amazing geometric models offered as tools for healing. The stall was run by a man and a woman dressed in saffron robes with all the tools being handmade by western Buddhist monks in America.

Having practised Buddhist meditation and studied these teachings for many years, I could not understand how these tools had anything to do with either of them. As I allowed my eyes to absorb the structures, my heart opened to embrace the fundamental Truth held within each one; these were three dimensional, sacred mandalas.

As is my want, I came away with a car load (or so it seemed to my house and my bank balance!) and sacred 3D mandalas can now be found hanging at strategic points around my house, including a six foot star tetrahedron meditation pyramid in the garden. I cannot deny the positive changes that have occurred in my life since bringing these tools to my home. The changes are all very subtle; I and my life have shifted to another level, another vibration, as a result.

The 'co-incidences' became more incredible from that point onwards. I went to a 'splodge' day at a friend's home where we played at throwing paint onto paper (the result of one of these 'splodges' became the 'Inner Alchemy' drawing some six months later) and took along one of my sacred geometry 'tools' to share with the group. To cut a long story short, one person said "if you want to know about Sacred Geometry you should contact the Flower of Life organisation". Two days later a DVD arrived containing an interview with Drunvalo Melchizedek discussing the teachings of Sacred Geometry.

All he conveyed made perfect sense to me in a very simple and profound way. On viewing the website I found there to be a Flower of Life merkaba meditation workshop two weeks hence and only a twenty minute journey from my brother in the north east of England. There were two places left! The merkaba meditation has been my daily practise for over two years. My understanding of Sacred Geometry, of ancient teachings and of life itself has expanded along with my consciousness ever since.

In August 2007 I joined a week-long sacred geometry retreat with Ron and Lyssa Holt, directors of Flower of Life Research, USA. Having participated in numerous retreats, with different teachers delivering many aspects of ancient wisdom over several years, I can honestly say this was the most profound, uplifting, and empowering experience I had ever participated in. Simple geometric shapes awakened profound understanding of cosmic proportion whilst experiential exercise opened my heart to reach deep levels of acceptance that I could not even have touched upon in my wildest dreams.

Following the retreat, within a period of eight short months, 18 drawings based on the principles of Sacred Geometry, including the one that transcended 'the system' came into being. The 'Light' set had been born. Whereas the 'Love' set had been about embracing and remembering all that was the 'golden age', this created a bridge to the highest aspects of being right here and right now; integrating the most pure vibrations of light into ordinary everyday life.

The poems also had a different flow and feel to them; more simple and easier to interpret yet embedded within was profound depth and clarity. I had been having difficulties finding words to create verse, my mind seemed to get in the way and tried to make things 'fit'. Words didn't flow with the same ease as creating drawings. I had never even liked poetry let alone written it so this was quite a stumbling block for me.

Another co-incidence led me to a lady who channelled the energy of Christ Consciousness. Again, like the yoga show, it was not something I would normally be drawn to yet I felt impelled to go. During the 'reading', I asked for help with the project, in particular the poems, and was given the name of a being who would assist. Although I have a name by which I call for his help, he wishes to remain anonymous and desires no credit for the part he plays in manifesting this work. I shall refer to him as 'the Silent One' and I am immensely grateful for the tremendous service he provides. He enables the most profound and expansive states of awareness to be expressed in very simple, fluid and easy to understand ways.

Previous poems had been written under the influence of Thoth, the Atlantean, for he was a huge influence during my contemplations at the time. Written in 'old English' they required space for the meaning to become clear. I had considered rewriting them but realise they are still very much valid. They are as much a part of your journey and unfoldment as they were (and still are) to mine.

Thoth was the founder/inventor of writing, drawing and Sacred Geometry. In a later life he was known as Hermes Trismegistus meaning 'thrice great'. The wisdom of his teaching invites the seeker to break through the boundaries of space and time. He is an inspiring being, transmitting profound understanding of cosmic magnitude through his wisdom, and will appeal to any seeker who desires to know the most profound truth lying at the heart of existence. I love his timeless teachings and contemplate them still.

It was October 2008 when the Visions Project ground to a halt. It entered the great void and was not to emerge for some thirteen months. The artwork was complete, forty visions, along with sixteen of the accompanying poems and part of this introduction, yet there was nothing more. I had no choice but to let go.

Other avenues of creative opportunity were being made available with lengthy articles materialising following research into ancient wisdom; Kabbalah, Chakra system, the Seven Rays, Esoteric Astrology and naturally Sacred Geometry, most of which had fired my soul since early teens.

Running parallel to and acting as a container for this river of research arose a deepening appreciation of all that was natural and ordinary in my everyday life. Maybe, for the first time, I began to enjoy, really enjoy, life on planet earth. Profound spiritual insight would emerge whilst enjoying the company of friends and family even though 'spirituality' was definitely not the agenda. Sanctity of ordinariness filled my days with reverent appreciation whilst understanding blossomed into a marriage of perfection in my continuing research.

In August 2009, whilst lunching with some friends, another 'chance' meeting occurred, this with a lady who played a large part in my healing process some ten years earlier whilst I was still a very stressed out air traffic controller.

To cut a long story short, after two or three social meetings, I offered to share the Visions Project including the 'block' I had to writing more poems and to completing the work. I had so many ideas, the images connected easily to the systems I had been researching, but it all seemed so huge and I had no idea as to where to begin the process of integrating it all. In a few short minutes, as creative energy flowed between us, clarity emerged and the picture was transformed.

The essence of 'Visions of Reality' is to connect, through contemplation, with the inner teacher; to awaken the light of Truth and understanding from within. An excess of knowledge contained within its pages would only cloud the simple clarity revealed within each vision.

A complete rehash ensued. In reviewing all the material I had researched, contemplated and accumulated I realised everything needed to complete the book was right under my nose. For at least six months it was actually complete. I just couldn't see it – no wonder there was nothing more coming through!

As a result, the poems have now become 'Seed Thoughts' which offer a tantalising taste of Truth to lead you on a journey of self discovery. Each thought is derived from one of the original sixteen poems, nine of which are printed in their entirety to entice you into deeper avenues of exploration.

Connection with ancient wisdom and systems of knowledge is restricted to their simple essence revealing enough for the seeker to detect the threads of light that run through them all. As these threads weave their way through the tapestry of everyday life, a glorious picture emerges reflecting the entirety of existence; the totality of All That Is.

One final twist to the journey came when I began researching avenues for publication. My vision of a pack of contemplation cards began to slowly diminish as I awoke to the difficulties of not only publishing but also selling a product in this form to a wide audience, particularly as an unknown author. I warmed to the idea of initially releasing the work as a full colour book with the cards following later as additional resources for contemplation. This way it could be on the shelves and distributed globally with the minimum of fuss in a matter of months. With natural ease the final stage of the journey was following in a similar manner to the river of creative force that had delivered it in the first place.

Naturally a rewrite ensued that the product may lend itself to ease of use in book format. The 'suits' became 'sets', cards became 'visions' with images, seed thoughts and symbols arranged in such a way that all may be contemplated from a simple two page spread. Once I had integrated these changes, the rest of the book simply fell into place and the rest, as they say, is history.

I realise life is a journey, a process. In adopting willingness to change and releasing my attachment to fixed agendas throughout its entirety the 'Vision' has followed its own course into reality. Through contemplation and review of this process the light of Truth shines through the darkness of separation; disparate parts come together, the self is complete, and the world is a better place as a result.

'Visions of Reality' offers unique opportunity to integrate your personality with your soul, to consciously re-create a golden age where all is absolute perfection and all is light. May the wisdom of understanding illuminate your days and truth be the master of your life.

42 Visions – is it significant?

At the last minute two additional drawings ('A Point of Light' and 'Illumination'), apparently unconnected with this project, were birthed and only after researching numerological implications did I realise they must be included.

In order to understand the significance of number 42 it necessitates taking it apart to examine the components comprising its entirety (this act alone offers some foresight into its relevance). These can be seen to comprise the following:

40+2, 10x4=40, 4+2=6, 6x7=42

The essential numbers to consider are, therefore:

0, 1, 2, 4, 6, 7, 10, and 40

Zero, seen three times in the sequence above, is the cosmic egg, the Great Void where all things exist in a state of non-existence. One (also seen three times) symbolises unity and is the primal cause for the manifestation of duality; it is the masculine creative principle and an expression of Divine Will. Two is duality and is the two fold nature of the human being. It is the feminine principle, Divine Love, and represents all that is separate within earthly experience. Interestingly it appears twice.

Displayed four times, the number four is the first solid number and equates to the foundation of earth. There are four cardinal points in a compass; four seasons and four elements (earth, air, fire and water); four sides to a square; four arms to a cross.

Six is the number of harmony and equilibrium, a fusion of two interlocking triangles to form a six pointed star. The triad itself finds the underlying unity between disparate parts so this becomes a powerful unifying force for integrating opposites including that of spirit with matter.

Seven brings in Absolute perfection; it is the number of the Holy Spirit being the three of the eternal triad and the four of physical existence. There are seven ages of man, seven rays of God, seven chakras, seven wonders of the ancient world, seven days of the week, the list is endless; its spiritual significance cannot be ignored.

Ten is the number of completion. Known as the Decad it contains all other digits and is therefore all things and all possibilities. It is the one and the zero and unifies masculine and feminine principles breaking down to a single digit; the 'one' symbolising unity. Ten is all inclusive and follows the natural order of the universe; cosmic law and order.

Forty, being the four and the ten, unifies the solidity of matter with natural order and completion. It indicates consummation of one way of being to enter an entirely new level of existence. The inner meaning of 40 is to see ascent from one level to the next as did Christ following the 40 days he spent in the wilderness. However the attainment of the higher can only be achieved through completion of the lower, signified by the number ten in this combination. The zero in this configuration shows a necessity for surrender of the old and descent into the Great Void, to allow deliverance of something entirely new.

All this considered, being the totality of all the aforementioned digits, 42 signifies a new creation unified by the sum of all parts from a previous way of being; a very fitting expression for the intention behind 'Visions of Reality'.

Missing Numbers

In reviewing this chapter I feel it pertinent to consider the missing numbers, whether they are significant, and if so what are their implications? I will begin by looking deeper into the elements contained within the 'Visions of Reality – *Art of Synthesis*' project, including the numerology associated with the name itself, to determine its validity as a holistic work of art. The missing digits are: 3, 5, 8 and 9.

Beginning with the name itself, numbers are assigned to letters as follows:-

1	2	3	4	5	6	7	8	9
A	B	C	D	E	F	G	H	I
J	K	L	M	N	O	P	Q	R
S	T	U	V	W	X	Y	Z	

'Visions of Reality' expressed as number is:

VISIONS: 4+9+1+9+6+5+1=35. 3+5=8
OF: 6+6=12. 1+2=3
REALITY: 9+5+1+3+9+2+7=36. 3+6=9

Therefore 'Visions of Reality' is made up of the numbers 8, 3, and 9 which when added together are: 8+3+9=20 resulting in the single digit, 2.

'Art of Synthesis' is as follows:

ART: 1+9+2=12. 1+2=3
OF: 6+6=12. 1+2=3
SYNTHESIS: 1+7+5+2+8+5+1+9+1=39. 3+9=12. 1+2=3

This truly lives up to its title being made up of 3x3 (balance and harmony), totalling 9, the number of perfection.

And so, we have found three of our four missing numbers. Number three, found in both combinations of letters, number eight from the word 'visions' and number 9 as a digital expression of 'Reality' as well as being the sum digit in 'Art of Synthesis'.

The only missing digit is the number five, which I will come to later. Now I shall focus on the qualities of the new digits we have found, beginning with the number three.

Three is the number of harmony. It is the tripartite nature of the universe being body, soul and spirit; birth, life and death; beginning, middle and end etc. Three is a complete cycle in itself and overcomes duality by moving the energy to a point of synthesis. Aside from the correlations mentioned above, it is particularly relevant being the totality of the Sets. Their associated attributes are also threefold in nature.

Eight is attributed to the word 'vision' at the core of this work, and is the symbol for infinity. It represents continuation, repetition and evolutionary cycles. Eight is divisible by 1, 2 and 4 and weaves together the principles of unity, polarity and materialisation. When repeatedly halved, it arrives at the number one, unity.

Nine is a powerful combination 3x3, three trinities, the triple triad, and is considered a very sacred number. It signifies completion being the last number before unity is reached at the decad. When any number is multiplied by nine, the sum of its parts, always add up to nine (e.g. 9x7=63 6+3=9, 9x6=54 5+4=9). Nine will always reproduce itself and return to itself whilst, at the same time, embracing every other number on its way. *'Art of Synthesis'* embodies these principles, as well as the digits, and illustrates the sacred nature of this work.

This completes the analysis of numbers associated with this work. As you can see, there is still no occurrence of the number five. Does this mean it has no relevance? Let's examine it and see.

Number Five

Positioned at the centre of our journey from one to ten, five is the number of the human being. It is the number of life itself, the pentad, pentagram and five pointed star. A circular number, reproducing itself when raised to its own power (5x5=25), it is also the origin of the dodecahedron (consisting of 12 pentagrams), the most circular of the five platonic solids. Number five raises the vibration of number four (matter) to another level by giving it life.

In order for spirit to create new life it must destroy old forms. This natural order is illustrated admirably through the relationship of five to four. The formula: 5=4+1 explains how a blade of grass will break through concrete to create new life. It is able to do so because the number of life (five) is always stronger than that of matter (four) as it contains absolute energy, symbolised by the number one.

This digit, lying at the centre of our known universe, is obviously of paramount importance, for it holds within it the secret of life itself. Why then does it not play a part within the pages of this book? The answer lies in its essential essence 'life', and life in the case of 'Visions of Reality' is you, the reader. It is the relationship **you** have with all the material held within its pages that enables the old form to be transformed and taken forward into your world, to create your reality. YOU, quite literally, breathe life into the form. In conjunction with you, the life aspect, 'Visions of Reality – *art of synthesis'* encompassing every digit, really is a holistic and sacred work of art.

How to use this book

First of all I will begin with some general advice on the structure of this work. As well as the image, the symbol for the relevant set is displayed on the opposite page along with its title and corresponding seed thought. Specific information concerning connection to the Tree of Life and corresponding Chakra is displayed within the tables and diagrams on pages 128-131. If you wish to gain understanding of the ancient wisdom associated with each image, it is highly recommended you begin by studying these pages following selection of your 'vision'.

The primary message of this work, however, is to awaken the teacher within that personality and soul may function as one integrated presence. I would therefore offer one piece of advice: KEEP IT SIMPLE!

The language of the soul is sincere, naked and pure. It is the ego that likes to complicate things. Abundant means of communication exist within the image, symbol and seed thought to establish a lifetime of communion with the most divine aspects of your being.

I must nevertheless acknowledge that, without my ego desire to research ancient wisdom, this project would never have left the ground so there is definitely merit in following these lines of enquiry. Added to which study and reflection upon ancient wisdom, held within spiritual teachings, opens the heart to understanding through ever increasing clarity of mind. This in itself is soul integration. Subsequent to the chapters on the visions, in the closing pages, is a brief synopsis of three systems. A good understanding of these three systems will enable a deeper resonance with soul purpose.

Next I will provide a short introduction on the art of contemplation to help you to gain the most from your chosen image or symbol.

Contemplation

The art of contemplation requires space and time. It is not something to be rushed or manipulated. Start with watching the breath and bring your attention to the pause in between the in and out breath. Continue to breathe normally with relaxed focus; this creates space and allows your mind to slow down. It is important not to have any agenda. You are simply watching and breathing. As you continue to observe, allow yourself to become the 'pause' - simply merge with its presence. At this point you can relax your attention on the breath.

Abide in a position of relaxed focus and allow the object of contemplation, (image, seed thought or symbol etc.) to arise gently in your mind. In the case of image allow your gaze to softly alight upon its form and notice any thoughts, feelings or insights that appear. Again don't fixate on or try to manipulate any of these impressions; simply allow them to come and go.

If nothing happens or if you loose your focus LET IT GO. This is really important. Allow the object of reflection to move to the back of your mind and get on with your daily life. I find going for a walk or taking a shower helps to move the energy; before long you will find clarity and insight appearing from nowhere. Reading the section on 'Daath' (p133) will help in understanding this creative process.

Finally it is important to write down your insights. Understanding gained from contemplation rarely happens in one sitting. It evolves and grows and bears fruit over time. Keeping a diary of your insights will enable you to follow your own process of integration.

Life is a journey, a process and, by the same token, so is 'Visions of Reality'. Selection of an image is an invitation for you to take the first step on this journey. Should you choose to accept, it will guide you through the pages of this book to touch levels of your being that you have never before encountered. Every step you take finds all that is false gradually fade to nothing, allowing the light of your soul to emerge naturally from within. As understanding of this process filters into your daily life, it is transformed. It radiates outwards, in ever increasing circles, to enrich the lives of others. Thus cosmic understanding intertwines with earthly existence, YOUR existence. This is the beauty of 'Visions of Reality', it is the *Art of Synthesis*; One Vision, One journey, One life. The following suggestion is offered to assist you in taking your first step with an example of a full 'visions' experience provided at the end of this chapter.

One Vision, One Journey...

Soul integration is a sacred act so maximum benefit will be obtained if you make a ritual of selecting your image. Find a quiet space where you will not be disturbed (this can be outside in nature), bring your mind to a contemplative state using the techniques mentioned above, and set your intention for selecting the vision. Lighting a candle will help focus your attention on the 'light' aspect of your being. The method of selecting an image can vary. Here are three suggestions:

1. Hold the book at your heart whilst setting the intention in your mind then randomly open the book at an image.

2. Browse through the chapters containing the visions and notice any that jump out at you. Also notice those that you feel a definite aversion to; these may be just the images you need at this moment!

3. Contemplate the 'Visions of Reality' symbol (p33), notice which aspect draws your attention, and then select an image from the corresponding set. If the symbol in its entirety holds your attention then turn to the section 'Beyond all Systems' and follow its guidance.

If more than one image is prominent, gradually refine your selection until only one remains. If it is not possible to do this, then work with each one individually following the same methodology. A pattern will emerge giving a broader perspective or offering more than one avenue of approach to your issue. I would place a maximum limit of three cards, when working in this way, allowing plenty of time in between each one, so the different avenues of exploration may be fully absorbed into your understanding.

Now allow the image to sink into your awareness. Approaching it with childlike curiosity will let your imagination lead you on a journey which can often bring quite surprising results. The image may be all that is needed at this stage.

Understanding may then be expanded by contemplating the seed thought followed by the symbol associated with the set. The key attributes of the set and its corresponding seed thought take you to the next stage on your inner journey. Use the table and diagrams mentioned above to locate the image within the Tree of Life. Its related chakra and geometry will also be apparent. These offer further avenues of exploration and subsequent enquiries lead to its connecting paths, spheres, chakras or geometries. Use the index to locate the pages containing additional information on each element. These are the signposts on your journey.

Do not rush this process. As the example illustrates, the journey from image to integration involves many steps. You will gain the most if you pause and contemplate **each one** before moving onto the next. The importance of writing down, not only the images at each step, but also your initial enquiry along with personal insights etc, cannot be over emphasised. You will gain the most and facilitate ease of integration if you follow this advice.

The Systems

This method is included for seekers who have knowledge of ancient wisdom and wish to deepen their understanding of the systems specifically connected with this work.

Tree of Life

Using the diagrams featured on pages 130/131, select an image situated within the tree; the paths may be seen as the branches with the spheres the flowers. Contemplate the image, seed thought, symbol and poem associated with each sphere/path. The fruits materialise as you awaken understanding of the subtle energies flowing throughout. Known as 'pathworking' in kabbalistic circles, it offers a unique way of working with the subtle energies contained within the tree and as such within your own being. This is a life long journey!

Chakras

A similar technique may be applied when working with the chakras. Using the diagram on page 147, make your selection, focusing on a chakra beforehand, then contemplate the energies presented. As well as the section on 'Chakras', the chapter 'Art of Synthesis' contains many insights into the interrelations between each one and their affinities to the Tree of Life and Sacred Geometry.

Traditional Tarot Spreads

The images may easily adapt to any of the traditional tarot spreads. I find the following to be of particular relevance, being in tune with the vibration of this work.

Tetractys

The Tetractys is a triangular figure consisting of ten points arranged in four rows as shown in the graphic below. It is a mystical symbol and was very important to the Pythagorean mystery schools.

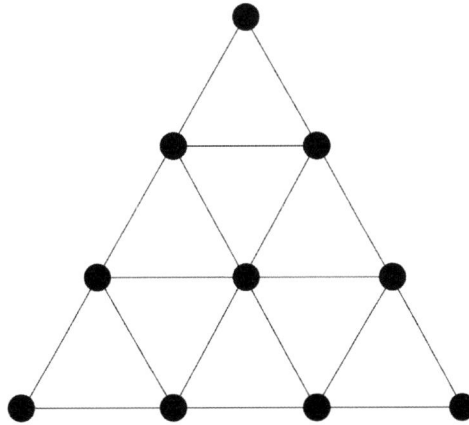

First Row: Represents the Premise of the reading forming a foundation for the understanding of all the other cards.

Second Row: Represents the cosmos and the individual and their relationship.

- The Light Card to the right represents the influence of the cosmos leading the individual to an action
- The Dark Card to the left represents the reaction of the cosmos to the actions of the individual

Third Row: of three positions represents three kinds of decisions the individual must make.

- The Creator Card is rightmost representing new decisions and directions that may be made
- The Sustainer Card is in the middle representing decisions to keep balance and things that should not change
- The Destroyer Card is leftmost representing old decisions and directions that should not be continued

Fourth Row: represents the four Greek elements

- The Fire Card is rightmost representing dynamic creative force, ambitions and personal will
- The Air Card is to the right middle representing the mind, thoughts, and strategies toward goals
- The Water Card is to the left middle representing the emotions, feelings and whims
- The Earth Card is leftmost representing physical realities of day to day living.

(http://en.wikipedia.org/w/index.php?title=Special:Cite&page=Tetractys&id=335160732)

Sample Journey (easily adaptable to all of the above methods)

Question: What do I need to enhance my life right now?

Selected image: **Rainbow Bridge**

Seed thought: *"Moments sublime see expressions unfold,*
in each precious instant the story is told"

Set: 'Power' **Seed thought**: "Be the Change" **Attributes**: Will, Strength

Symbol: Star Tetrahedron

Tree of Life: Path 14 (Empress: Wholeness/Creativity) linking Wisdom (Divine Inspiration) and Understanding (Divine Darkness)

Chakra: Brow (Creative Thought)

Geometry: Seed of Life

Additional Set: 'Light' "Every Thought is your Prayer". **Symbol**: 'Wave'

Interpretation

Image: Rainbow Bridge

The easiest and most obvious way to contemplate an image is to say what you see. This will be different each time you view it and will vary with every viewer.

"On first glance I see a window to another world. Bubbles of light lead me in, as do the two dogs playing on the right side of the picture. A gentle stream takes me deeper and leads me up the valley to the shafts of light, bursting from behind the distant fells. As my eyes are drawn to the sky, an ordinary journey is transformed; it becomes somewhat surreal. All is not as it seems. Another window has appeared and this is in the sky itself. The shafts of light I had believed to be emanating from behind the fells now originate from some far distant land lying beyond a new window.

I stand transfixed. I realise the world I had thought to be solid and real is but a bubble just like all the other bubbles that frame this picture. Suddenly, I find myself on the inside looking out. How would it be if I were to look through

the window of another bubble? What exciting new worlds could I explore? What would happen if I danced along this glorious rainbow and allowed the two playful dogs to lead me from one bubble to the next? I am filled with joy and excitement. What fun it would be! Again I pause and stand transfixed. What if I am the creator of these bubbles? What would happen if I stepped into a world that was of my own creation? ..."

Seed thought:

"Moments sublime see expressions unfold,
in each precious instant the story is told"

"...the story continues as I allow the words to permeate my being. What if I am actually standing, and even living, in this world I have created? Maybe time itself is within these bubbles...

...a distant memory finds its way into this present moment. The border collie racing, with such gay abandon through the annals of time and space, is no other than my old friend 'Buster' who passed on some five years ago (almost to the day). I feel strangely comforted and recall the wonderful times we shared, the mountains we climbed, during the 17 years we were together on this earth. He returns once more, fractures the bubble of separation I had created since his passing, and leads me deep into my heart to touch the part that knows only love. All sense of separation dissolves as does time itself. There is only this present moment. That is all there is. There is nothing else. What I do, how I am, and how I respond in each moment creates my reality. And in this present moment there is unity, all that was lost is found, all that was broken is whole and all that was pain is love. Thank you Buster."

Set: 'Power' **Seed thought**: "Be the Change" **Attributes**: Will, Strength

"These qualities bring a change of energy. I feel a sense of purpose. Strength and Will permeate my being to penetrate even the most dense aspect, my physical body. Every cell is energised. This purpose carries with it responsibility. It is a call for action, effort, and the only one who can perpetuate its motion is me. "Be the Change" embodies power, purpose. It seems 'change' is afoot and the only way to embrace it is to 'be' it. Now that does give me a sense of purpose!"

Symbol: Star Tetrahedron

"My sense of power and purpose has softened with the introduction of this symbol. The all-embracing wisdom of my heart, awakened through the memory of my old friend, brings with it the gift of love. Love, Will and Power are very potent principles for embodying change, they enable respons-ability. I am able to act from my authentic self with love, integrity and purpose. This is soul integration, the union of masculine and feminine, love and power, spirit and matter."

Completion of these four steps sees the first stage of the journey complete. This may be sufficient for the time being, particularly for those who are new to this process. Either way, my suggestion is to allow a period of time before moving on to explore the systems.

Tree of Life: Path 14 (Wholeness/Creativity) linking Wisdom (Divine Inspiration) and Understanding (Divine Darkness)

"As soon as I connect with this path and its position on the Tree of Life, I am elevated to the region between my eyebrows. I stand at the centre, a bridge between two mighty forces, Light (Divine Inspiration) and Dark (Divine Darkness), each one a mirror of the other. Neither one sways me to their cause. I am simply a bridge that is the union of these two apparent opposites. However, each in their turn exerts influence presenting opportunity to experience reflections of divinity. Wisdom and understanding develop with each cyclic turn of events, the mighty bridge is strengthened, and two become One."

Chakra: Brow (Creative Thought)

All that has gone before has been direct experience of the energies presented. Arrival at the brow chakra sees this journey culminate in intellectual reasoning, for this chakra, as well as being one of the intuition, also holds the qualities of analytical knowledge and science. Both the lower and higher mind reside here, the bridge between the two being known as the Antakarana or Rainbow Bridge. As the keywords suggest, it is the centre of creative thought, its full potential only being realised if the lower mind succumbs to the higher, just as the personality becomes the servant of the soul. The intellectual mind is important, and has its place but, as is so often the case in the western world, it frequently rules the roost. This has to change. As the preceding journey shows, we have to connect with our feeling nature and marry this with intellectual understanding. This will enable 'thinking from the heart', the prelude to creative thought and the use of the higher mind.

Geometry: Seed of Life

"This geometry holds within it the seed of all creation. It expands through ever increasing rounds of concentric circles to produce the flower and ultimately the fruit of life." In the context of this illustration it may be seen in the light of 'as you sow, so shall you reap'. How you are in each moment echoes through time and space to create your reality. Whatever seeds you sow, whether positive or negative, **will** bear fruit over time. Just as an acorn will never mature into a willow neither will a negative thought produce a positive outcome. It really is that simple.

Additional Set: 'Light' "Every Thought is your Prayer". **Symbol**: 'Wave'

This aspect is included as, through the Tree of Life, our selected vision connects two visions from this set. In fact, **every vision in all three sets** will lead, eventually, to the 'Light'. Now there is an uplifting thought!

"The most profound and yet the simplest of all the elements, the wave is the river of Truth that cannot be contained by any structure yet is in absolute intimacy with all. It is the pre-eminent spark that gives birth to all realities and expressions." This river carries the seed thought 'every thought is your prayer' into reality and sets the tone for the manifestation of all that is your highest aspiration, should you choose to create this. The set 'guidance' offers profound insight into the power of thought and instructs you to 'be the master architect of your life'. "Be aware. Become your prayer, and create!"

Understanding

"Once more the image is reflected on the surface of my mind. This time it appears, quite spontaneously during meditation, one day after completing the sequence of events above. I am inside the picture, at the point where distant fells turn to greet the opening in the sky. I adjust my head in accord, my crown chakra opens to receive the light from beyond, and all is bathed in its radiance. Clear light of Truth, married with intellectual knowledge, carries the gift of clear-seeing and gives birth to knowing, inner knowing.

In re-visiting the image I am given direct experience of the 14th path, its two connecting spheres, and the refined energies of the brow chakra. Let me explain. When viewed within the Tree of Life, in linear form, the connections between path 14 (Rainbow Bridge) and the two spheres, Wisdom and Understanding, are clearly delineated. Association with the brow chakra is also obviously displayed. I may study these intellectually and even reach a deep level of understanding as to how each one interacts with the other but I will not have 'knowing' of them in a holistic sense.

*My experience during meditation allowed me to 'be' all of these elements simultaneously, the image acting to facilitate their synchronistic union: One vision, One viewer, One reality. The 'crater' was 'Divine Darkness', the divine feminine aspect, open to receive 'Divine Inspiration', the masculine creative impulse, whilst 'rainbow bridge' (subtle in nature) facilitated the flow of energy between the two. There was nothing linear in this interaction, each aspect played its part, and energy flowed naturally between them all. Knowledge of the brow chakra, and even the subtle workings of the physical brain, is also mirrored in this understanding. The left logical brain, and its intuitive counterpart on the right, are **both** essential in developing direct existential knowing.*

There are many golden nuggets running throughout this reading but its essential message, above all else, is to take responsibility. The vision and its seed thought has set in motion a chain reaction which, if acted upon, holds the potential for a new way of 'being' in the world. When one person takes responsibility for their corner of the world, unconditionally, it gives others permission to do the same. It begins with a thought, 'Divine Inspiration', which may hold within it a dream. This dream has the potential to become reality. After all Martin Luther King Jr. 'had a dream' and, nearly 50 years later, it has become reality for millions of people throughout the world. Such is the power of thought! The essence of this message is to **consciously create** your vision, your dream, and your life. Here lies the answer to the question posed at the beginning of this journey.

Further Exploration

Tree of Life/Chakras:

Centres of Creativity (p142) – Throat (Becoming), Sacral (Arcturus)

Triad – Divine Darkness/Divine Inspiration/Gnosis (brow/crown)

Triad – Divine Darkness/Divine Inspiration/Trust (brow/heart)

Triad – Apocalypse/Genesis/Arcturus (solar plexus/sacral)

Path 27 (Rebirth: Pride/Destruction/Revelation) between Apocalypse/Genesis

These connections are tabulated to show the depths to which you may travel following selection of a single vision. No matter what the outer circumstances, whatever the initial question or reason for turning to this resource, each selection will open a door through which you may experience new realities. How far you go on this journey is entirely up to you, there are no right or wrong ways. The paths you choose upon entering the Tree of Life (for instance) may be different to those outlined above. They are YOUR way, and your responsibility. It is your journey and only you can walk it. Use your imagination, your intuition, and explore. Walk with joy in your heart. 'Journeying' is fun!

About the Symbol

A marriage of all three sets through an equal number of elements - circle, star tetrahedron and wave – the symbol is in itself a powerful tool for contemplating aspects of reality. It is said 'a picture paints a thousand words' yet a symbol will paint a thousand pictures. It speaks the language of the soul and as such is a highly intuitive medium for awakening its light.

The only three dimensional aspect to the symbol, the **star tetrahedron** (see p137) is in essence a powerful tool for achieving harmony between opposing forces; spirit and matter, personality and soul, masculine and feminine etc. Although primarily a masculine solid, composed entirely of straight lines, the star tetrahedron nevertheless incorporates both masculine and feminine principles: the downward pointing triangle being feminine - matter, the upward masculine - spirit.

Closer examination finds nine smaller triangles within the whole. Nine is the number of pure intelligence representing Truth as it reproduces itself when multiplied. It is the Triple Triad - completion; fulfilment; attainment; beginning and the end. All this considered, the star tetrahedron aspect plays a major role in refining the personality as a perfected vehicle for soul expression; its importance at the heart of the symbol cannot be overstated.

Clearly feminine, the **circle** is the Great Void, the hidden sphere, in the Tree of Life. It is a space, a void, which holds within its centre infinite creative potential. It serves as a container for the star tetrahedron and facilitates ease of action during the process of integration. In Sacred Geometry it is the primal act of creation setting the foundation for the involution of spirit into matter and the subsequent evolutionary process of return. An intuitive understanding of its essence may be gained through reading the section on 'Daath' (p133).

The most profound and yet the simplest of all the elements, the **wave** is the river of Truth that cannot be contained by any structure yet is in absolute intimacy with all. Surpassing even the pure creative force of the Great Void it is the pre-eminent spark that gives birth to all realities and expressions.

Vibrations of light, sound, matter and spirit every conceivable emotion, feeling, perception is delivered by and will return to the wave. The integrated personality, being the united star tetrahedron and circle, is at once the wave and the particle; in each moment arising from and returning to its source.

About the Sets

There are three sets called Light; Love and Power. Specific details concerning individual sets are given within the set itself. The following is an overview of the system as a whole.

As the Visions Project began to unfold and understanding of its connections to ancient wisdom developed, I noticed consistent repetitions of the triad appearing throughout the texts. The supernal triad in all these traditions brings forth a marriage of polar opposites creating the divine child; the fruit of divine union.

Christianity sees this divine triad expressed in mother, father God or father, son and Holy Ghost; Taoist teachings generate yin, yang, Tao; in Buddhism the three jewels are Buddha, dharma, sangha; there are three pillars in the Tree of Life as well as the supernal triad – the creator (Crown) wisdom (masculine) and understanding (feminine); three primary rays emanate from the Divine Creator – Will or Power, Love-Wisdom and Active Intelligence. The list appears endless.

When each system is examined at its essential core there is no diversity; all are the same, simply reflections of one truth. The opening mantram, the Great Invocation, is a prayer for the establishment of a new world religion, a vision for a new age, the Age of Aquarius, which will see an end to the trials and tribulations of diversity whilst at the same time embracing them all. It heralds an era of peace where all diversities and individuals are accepted within one divine attribute; world service.

Light and Love and Power are potent principles for the establishment of this new era and essential to this project; they make most appropriate titles for the sets.

Light

Key Attributes

Symbol	Wave
Aspect	Mind
Ray	Active Intelligence
Quality	Divine Child
Subtle Body	Mental
Buddhist Three Jewels	Buddha
Taoist	Tao
Kabbalah	Pillar of Equilibrium

"Every Thought is Your Prayer"

This set calls on you to embrace the highest aspect of your being. The wave like nature, title and seed thought bear testament to the level of transformation that may be attained by embracing the energies held within each of the contemplation constituents - image, seed thought, poem and symbol.

Representing the mind of God, Buddha nature and the Ray of Active Intelligence, it offers the seeker an opportunity to swim in crystal clear water, elevating the personality from the seas of deep mental/emotional/physical turmoil it is accustomed to swimming in.

The Greek myths tell tales of one of their famous heroes, Hercules, who must complete several trials ordered by the Oracle at Delphi. These tasks, known as the Labours of Hercules, are symbolic of man on the path of soul integration, each labour being a particular battle with an aspect of his personality. One labour which is of particular relevance when attempting to understand the significance of this set of contemplations concerns the slaying of the nine-headed hydra; although known by this name it has, in fact, ten heads with the tenth being immortal.

Labour of Hercules – Nine-headed hydra

The loathsome beast had as its lair a cave, deep within a dark and dingy bog inaccessible by any ordinary means. Hercules was given two simple hints for overcoming the beast; *'we rise by kneeling'* and *'if you try to kill the beast by severing any of the nine mortal heads two more will grow in its place'*.

After a period of time, Hercules located the hydra and, dragging it from its lair, promptly severed one of its mortal heads. Naturally, as the Oracle had predicted, another two grew rapidly in its place. Hercules however learnt fast and realising the futility of his efforts, threw away his sword. Then, kneeling down deep in the bog, he lifted the beast high above his head. Before long it ceased to struggle as one by one the nine mortal heads withered and died. The one remaining head he buried beneath a rock, placing upon it his foot, that it may never again emerge into the light of day.

Significance of the labour - The nine mortal heads are the root delusions that man on the spiritual path must face and destroy with the tenth being the mind of awareness that is essential to cultivate in order to prevent the heads from resurfacing. The mortal heads and their corresponding bodies are as follows:-

Physical: *money, sex, comfort*

Emotional: *fear, hatred, desire*

Mental: *pride, separativeness, cruelty*

This simple tale holds the essence of this set with each aspect holding an opportunity for you to transcend the lower nature of your personality. You will not achieve this unless you **surrender**, lift the energy to a higher mental level (symbolised by Hercules lifting the hydra into the light of day where it could not survive) and cultivate a mind of awareness.

Although embodying and emphasising the middle pillar of the Tree of Life, it is in fact all three pillars, being every sphere, which again demonstrates the unifying aspect to this particular set. Therefore, if any one of these visions is selected for contemplation, I would suggest the intention be focused on the highest aspect of light you are capable of at any given moment. Destroy the hydra and be the multi-dimensional being of light that is your true nature.

Four images in this set have more than one aspect: Apocalypse, Devotion, Genesis and Gnosis.

Additional Guidance

To engage in the creative process is to offer yourself as a receptacle for the divine, thus spirit may flow through you unimpeded into form. Each image, seed thought and poem within this set is an invitation for you to enter the Great Void from which all forms are made manifest. They offer an opportunity for you to know this Great Mystery and to experience the wonders of this most fertile process.

Surrender every idea, thought or feeling of who you perceive yourself to be and enter the great ocean of infinite possibilities. It is time to take responsibility and BE the master architect of your life. Know every thought is your prayer and as such will become reality. Be aware. Become your prayer, and create!

As thought gave birth unto a word
Wondrous sound through heaven was heard
Sweet music filters through my ears
To touch a chord my heart can hear
As beauty woken from her sleep
I know joy in heaven's deep
Crystalline light sublime
Reveals Truth to end all time
For light gives way unto the dark
And symbols form, so soon to spark
Remembrance... of the Truth... I AM

Apocalypse ~ Fire

Fire of awareness consumes from within

Apocalypse ~ Water

Fires of your passion turn water to rage
A powerful tide kills all in its wake

Arcturus

Cycle by cycle Truth will agree
In silence and mystery a blind man will see

Becoming

In darkness I rest 'til I am no more
In womb of creation safe and secure
Paths, they seem many, twenty two in all
Linking the spheres that lead man to his soul
Hidden are the paths that lie beyond Tree
A veil of illusion obscures them from me
Stillness and silence reveals now, the key
In deepest dark glows Eye of All seeing
Darkest of dark; light of All Being
Seed of creation; unmanifest becoming

Celebration

Life in a box
A world ran by clocks
Where am I when silence knocks?
Tick tock, tick tock...

Devotion ~ Compassion

Devotion ~ Clarity

Devotion ~ Unity

No search and no seeker, no truth to be found
The way of Non-Being; Spirit unbound

Divine Darkness

Naked intelligence absorbs day and night
For each wears the cloak of power to unite

Divine Inspiration

Radiant pure light sacred sound creates
In silence it touches calling all to awake

If thought were a prayer and mind the conveyer
Then who am I, director or player?
Perhaps I am both, are they one and the same?
Each of them parts I play in a game
And what of this void? This place between thought
Where all things fill a space that is naught
Is it the pause between beats of my heart?
Stillness that speaks when worlds fall apart,
Or silence that rests in the space between words?
The sound of the sea, the call of the birds,
The cry of a child that longs to be heard,
Am I all of these things, perhaps even none?
And if I am a product of thought turned to form
Am I also the void from which it was born?

Freedom

Fear not little one... will you come?
Will you play? Will you enter the mystery?
And leave all for this day?

Genesis ~ Inception

The sound of the sea, the call of the birds
The cry of a child that longs to be heard
Am I all of these things, perhaps even none?

Genesis ~ Manifestation

If thought were a prayer and mind the conveyer
Then who am I, director or player?

Gnosis ~ Purity

Gnosis ~ Tranquillity

Gnosis ~ Intelligence

Light gives way unto the dark
And symbols form so soon to spark
Remembrance... of the Truth... I AM

Trust

Upon spiral I ride with trust as my guide
The light and the dark has no place to hide

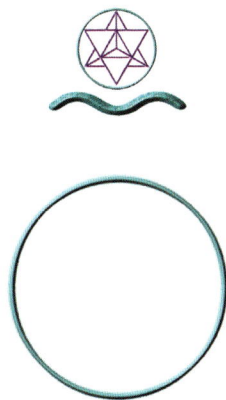

Love

Key Attributes

Symbol	Circle
Aspect	Heart of God
Ray	Love - Wisdom
Quality	Divine Mother
Subtle Body	Emotional
Buddhist Three Jewels	Sangha - Community
Taoist	Yin - Feminine
Kabbalah	Pillar of Compassion

"Let Go and Let God"

This set sees the emergence of the divine child. However, as the opening poem reveals, this may only come about through intense trial and apparent suffering on the part of the personality. Of the subtle bodies the emotional is the hardest to balance as it can often be open to manipulation, not only from others but also from the lower mind.

It is easy to drown in the depths of intense emotional drama so the slaying of the hydra is of equal relevance here as it was in the light set. All three poems displayed within this chapter have affinities with visions in the light set - Trust, Freedom and Devotion – so contemplation of these is also recommended in slaying your personal hydra.

The upside of this collection finds a river of gentle simplicity touching each page with soft golden light reflecting the true essence of the meaning behind its visions.

A million different connotations, complexities, and interpretations may be found within the four simple letters making up the word 'love' but lying at its heart, its pure essence, is a simple uncomplicated all-embracing wisdom of understanding; such is the love emanating from each of these visions should your heart be open to receive it.

And therein lays the key to working with this set. Open your heart, create a sacred space and allow the true essence of your own nature to arise gently from within. You have nothing to prove, nothing to achieve, nothing to become. Simply accept where you are, who you are with, however you are feeling, in each moment and suddenly you will find you are no longer there. This is the heart of wisdom.

Additional Guidance

There are many paths leading to the "Dark Night of the Soul". There appears to be no way out. The experience is one of absolute despair and aloneness. However, there is a way out and that way is you. **You** have to make a choice. Do you ride the spiral to peace or to despair? This set presents opportunity for you to "Let Go and Let God". Stop feeding your ego delusions and choose, instead, to embrace the glorious and wondrous being of light that you truly are!

Leading to your inner teacher, this set also invites you to explore polarity in your life. All relationships, including that of the student/guru, offer many benefits but their foundations lie in the realm of duality, where even devotion to God is polarised if God is perceived as being something external to the Self. Contemplate your sense of separativeness. Do you lead? Do you follow? Do you seek? Or do you teach? If there is a 'self' and 'a-nother' then your consciousness is polarised. In Unity Consciousness there may be one, two or even more 'selves' yet there is only one consciousness.

In darkest recess of mind I roam
With absence of light to guide my way home
Love, the betrayer has brought me to this
How fast have I fallen from ocean of bliss?
Spiral of darkness black hole of despair
The pain of this loss is too much to bear
So, my life I must take for no help is there
Fear grips my heart my soul torn asunder
Other steps I must take lest I go under
In this blackest of space, dark night of the soul
This hell of creation; I stand in NO MORE
I send forth a prayer with all of my might
From the depths of my being 'please show me the light'
Dawn of awaking brings forth revelation
Depths of despair are my own creation
Another turn of the spiral sees dark take new form
And I rest in deep space where knowing is born
Upon spiral I ride with trust as my guide
The dark and the light has no place to hide
Now brothers in arms, at my breast they reside

Chaos

Sweet music filters through my ears
To touch a chord my heart can hear

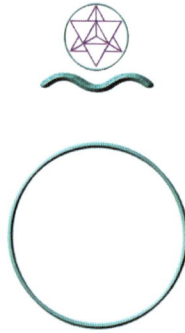

Creation

Dawn of awaking brings forth revelation
Seeds of compassion bear fruit in creation

Emergence

Naked and innocent a child of the morn
Fulfilling the purpose to which I am born

On the threshold of a dream she stands
Her feet as an anchor rest deep in the sand
As her eyes fill with longing and seek distant shore
She hears a sweet sound, tries hard to recall
Crash of the waves, birds flying high?
Or perhaps it's the sea as it touches the sky?
'Listen, listen... feel the vibration
Open your heart and accept invitation
For wisdom abounds in alien sound
With senses of light you see your salvation'
Come, come Little One, come play with me
Leave feet on the shore as one we'll explore
We'll swim through the seas and sail amongst stars
Beings we will greet as worlds become ours
By angles and spirals, through space and through time
Many realms we'll explore; an adventure sublime
So, fear not, Little One... Will you come? Will you play?
Will you enter the mystery, leave all for this day?

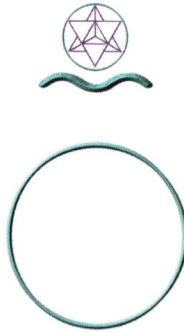

Empty Vessel

Self there is none... no self to impede
The veil of illusion will always mislead

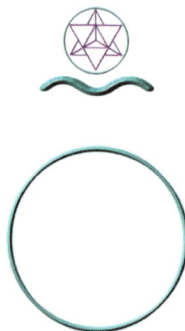

Eye Eye

The fall from existence gave birth to the fool
Mystery of spirit concealed in misrule
Dare you follow and go where he leads
Befriend the unknown, partake of the seed
And surrender your sight in order to see?

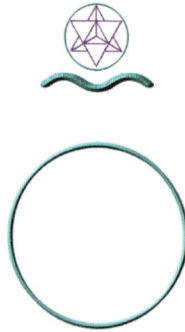

Mind

I withdraw to the centre merge with the whole
From time of beginning I am one and All

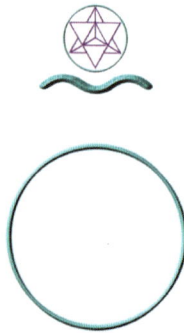

Phone Home

Alone he stands the star born
Isolation, loneliness companions of old

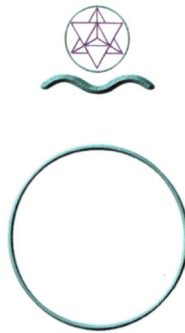

Recognition

Hello, little brother!
Friendship and brotherhood many times without form
Forever in service, fragments of One

With an eye to see and a heart to feel
The way of the seeker is clearly revealed
From time of beginning sought she for the Truth
Goal of long seeking to be Absolute
The path of devotion for aeons explored
Only to find this way to be flawed
Now eye of wisdom is opened and sees
Student with master forever will be
Trapped in this world of polarity
For love and devotion are simply emotions
Fuelled by desire and eternal salvation
Tis love of love that gives birth to devotion
A way of being that holds no emotion
As courage of wrath ignites divine fire
There is no self and no other to confuse with desire
No search and no seeker, no truth to be found
The way of Non-Being; spirit unbound

River of Souls

Rivers of life are a journey of the soul
Now time has come to leave all for the shore

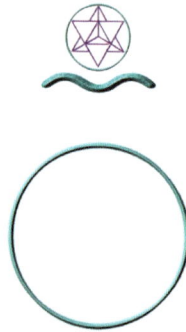

Unicorn

In heart of existence all wisdom and knowing
Is found in THIS moment of glorious awakening

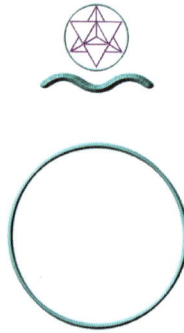

Welcome

As divine plan in my heart unfolds
I know perfection in myriad form

Power

Key Attributes

Symbol	Star Tetrahedron
Aspect	Will of God
Ray	Will and Power
Quality	Divine Father
Subtle Body	Physical/Etheric
Buddhist Three Jewels	Dharma - teachings
Taoist	Yang - masculine
Kabbalah	Pillar of Strength

"Be the Change"

Reflecting upon the key attributes of this set it is obvious the energy running through it is that of pure will. It is a set of action. The symbol alone demonstrates its high level of integration and the will and power needed to execute the changes necessary for its manifestation. The divine Father, the physical body, strength; everything about this set speaks of this earthly existence. Yet cosmic beings and journeys exude their light from within its pages. Clearly this is a meeting of spirit and matter, the ultimate integration. No wonder power is the driving force. But beware the power that drives this force is the Will of the Divine not that of the human being.

Additional Guidance

Life in the 21st century can often be serious and goal oriented. We spend our days dreaming of a better world, better relationships, more money, world peace and even spiritual enlightenment! This set is an invitation for you to wake up! Instead of standing on the shore wishing things would change, 'BE' the change. If you desire peace; 'BE' peace, happiness; 'BE' happy and if you seek enlightenment then 'BE' enlightened! It is time to step from the sidelines, join the game, and enter the Great Mystery that is the wonder of life itself. This **is** the whole new world of which you are dreaming!

An eye for an eye
A tooth for a tooth
Such is the wisdom of super sleuth
The Lord of Misrule plays man for a fool
As he dances through time to confuse and delude
The jester's disguise is laid bare to the wise
Behold him thus; see Truth and the lies
No-thing is he, just a clown with a part
Who plays the world game with joy in his heart
Naked and innocent a child of the morn
Fulfilling the purpose to which he was born
The fall from existence gave birth to the fool
Mystery of Spirit concealed in misrule
Dare you follow and go where he leads
Befriend the unknown, partake of the seed
And surrender your sight in order to see?
Have you the courage?
Dare you be free?

Alien Nation

Wisdom abounds in alien sound
Surrender all fear and touch the profound

Blank Canvas

And what of this void? This place between thought
Where all things fill a space that is naught

Family of Light

Listen, listen... feel the vibration
Open your heart and accept invitation

Inner Alchemy

Fires of your passion turn water to rage
A powerful tide swallows all in its wake
Whirlpool of anger destruction of all
To the bottomless depths sink all that you are
Extinguished the fire of your soul
For too long have these fires
Scorched waters of being
Now time has come to lay all to rest
Let waters be still, choose light for your guide
Well of compassion spread far and spread wide
Ignite now the fire of your soul
Hence forth, fire of your spirit moves upon water
Illuminates far, to the depths of your being
Water and fire divine union become
Each the same nature; the nature of One
Spirit of fire eternal in all
Fire of awareness consumes from within
Let fire burn bright and spirit will soar
Fountain of joy, divinity in all
Wonder of wonders, what radiance bright!
Primal quintessence new worlds to ignite

Jenny's Well

By angles and spirals through space and through time
Many realms to explore, an adventure sublime

Journey

From time of beginning sought she for the Truth
Goal of long seeking to be Absolute

Rainbow Bridge

Moments sublime see expressions unfold
In each precious instant the story is told

Rebirth

In darkness I rest until I am no more
In womb of creation, safe and secure

Alone he stands the star born
Isolation, loneliness companions of old
Too long has he walked these earth laden pathways
Spirit ever seeking a path to return
Long ago forgotten the race of the stars
Grown over time great love for this earth
Now he remembers, he remembers his calling
Sends forth a cry to the land of his birth
Returning swift the clan from afar
Embrace their brother, igniting his Light
As wisdom of ages flows through his being
A bridge he becomes twixt earth and the stars
Earth finds knowing of star born
Stars are wisdom of earth
Path to return established
At home on this land of his birth

Stillness

Seek eye of stillness at centre of storm
Know breath of your being flows through all

The Web

Moments in time seemingly without connection
Yet look to the web for each effect is not without its cause

Transmission

As thought gave birth unto a word
Wondrous sound through heaven was heard

About the 'Systems'

It does not fulfil the purpose of this book to provide a full functional analysis of the ancient wisdom associated with these visions, each one being a lifetime (at least) of study in its own right. The teachings within these traditions reveal timeless techniques for mastering the mind and achieving mental, emotional and physical harmony. I believe, therefore, a brief overview of three systems to be an integral part of this work, serving as synthesising agents for personality and soul integration

Each system provides a structure, a container, through which the river of life may flow. They are by no means absolute, both structure and river being parts within an even greater whole. I offer a brief explanation as to the function, form and position of the energies and the role they play in the unfolding of man's evolution towards self-realisation. The connections below result from research derived from many sources: books, internet, retreats, workshops, and courses etc. Above all they are an alliance derived through contemplation and meditation upon the results of these findings. I leave it to the reader to determine the validity of these understandings when considered against the environment of their own experience.

Kabbalah SPHERES, Chakras, Geometry and 'Visions' Correspondences

No.	SPHERE	CHAKRA	GEOMETRY	VISION of REALITY
1	Crown	Crown	Fruit of Life/Stellated Dodecahedron	Gnosis
2	Wisdom	Brow	Seed of Life/Tree of Life/Stellated Icosa	Divine Darkness
3	Understanding	Brow	Seed of Life/Tree of Life/Stellated Icosa	Divine Inspiration
0	Higher Knowledge	Throat	Vesica Piscis/Seed and Tree of Life	Becoming
4	Mercy	Heart	Dodecahedron/Stellated Dodecahedron	Devotion
5	Judgement	Heart	Octahedron	Freedom
6	Beauty	Heart	Spiral	Trust
7	Desire	Solar Plexus	Icosahedron	Genesis
8	Intellect	Solar Plexus	Star Tetrahedron	Apocalypse
9	Foundation/Illusion	Sacral	Seed of Life/Flower of Life	Arcturus
10	Manifestation/ Kingdom	Base	Cube	Celebration

Kabbalah PATHS, Tarot Archetypes and 'Visions' Correspondences

PATH	TAROT ARCHETYPES	KEYWORDS	VISION of REALITY
11	The Fool	Simplicity	Eye Eye
12	The Magician	Creative Thought	Transmission
13	The High Priestess	Wisdom/Receptivity	Chaos
14	The Empress	Wholeness/Creativity	Rainbow Bridge
15	The Star	Humility/Silence	Creation
16	The Hierophant	Unknowable Truth/No self	Blank Canvas
17	The Lovers	Discrimination	Recognition
18	The Chariot	Awareness	Welcome
19	Strength	Surrender/Inner Strength	Unicorn
20	The Hermit	Aloneness/Silence/Acceptance	Alien Nation
21	The Wheel of Fortune	Commitment/Opportunity/Cycles	Journey
22	Justice	Responsibility/Cause and Effect	The Web
23	The Hanged Man	Understanding/Change of View	Phone Home
24	Death	Illumination/Transformation/New Life	River of Souls
25	Temperance/Alchemy	Heal Thyself/Integration	Inner Alchemy
26	The Devil	Temptation/Purification	Stillness
27	Struck Tower	Pride/Destruction/Revelation	Rebirth
28	The Emperor	Natural Intelligence/Clear Seeing	Family of Light
29	The Moon	Illusion/Imagination/Reflection	Mind
30	The Sun	Innocence/Realisation	Emergence
31	Judgement	Beyond Illusion/Clarity/Renewal	Empty Vessel
32	The World	Universal Truth/Success	Jenny's Well
	Beyond all Systems	Enlightened Human/Ordinariness	A Walk in the Park
		"	Illumination
		"	A Point of Light

Visions of Reality

Tree of Life and Chakra
Correspondences

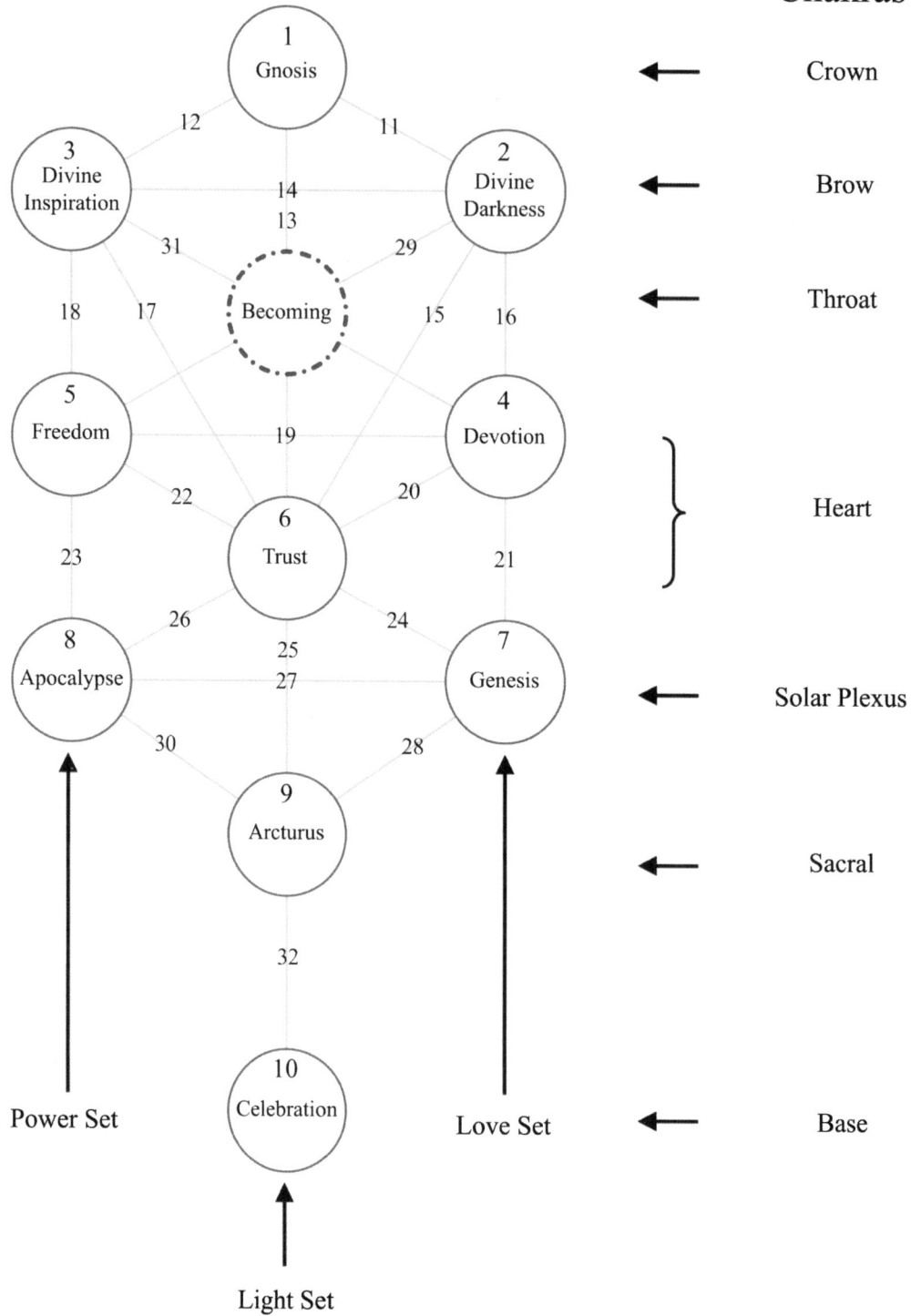

Chakras

1
Gnosis

← Crown

12   11

3
Divine
Inspiration

2
Divine
Darkness

← Brow

14
13

31   29

Becoming

18   17

15   16

← Throat

5
Freedom

4
Devotion

19

22

6
Trust

20

Heart

23

21

26

24

8
Apocalypse

25
27

7
Genesis

← Solar Plexus

30

28

9
Arcturus

← Sacral

32

Power Set

10
Celebration

Love Set

← Base

Light Set

Kabbalah

Tree of Life and Chakra
Correspondences

Chakras

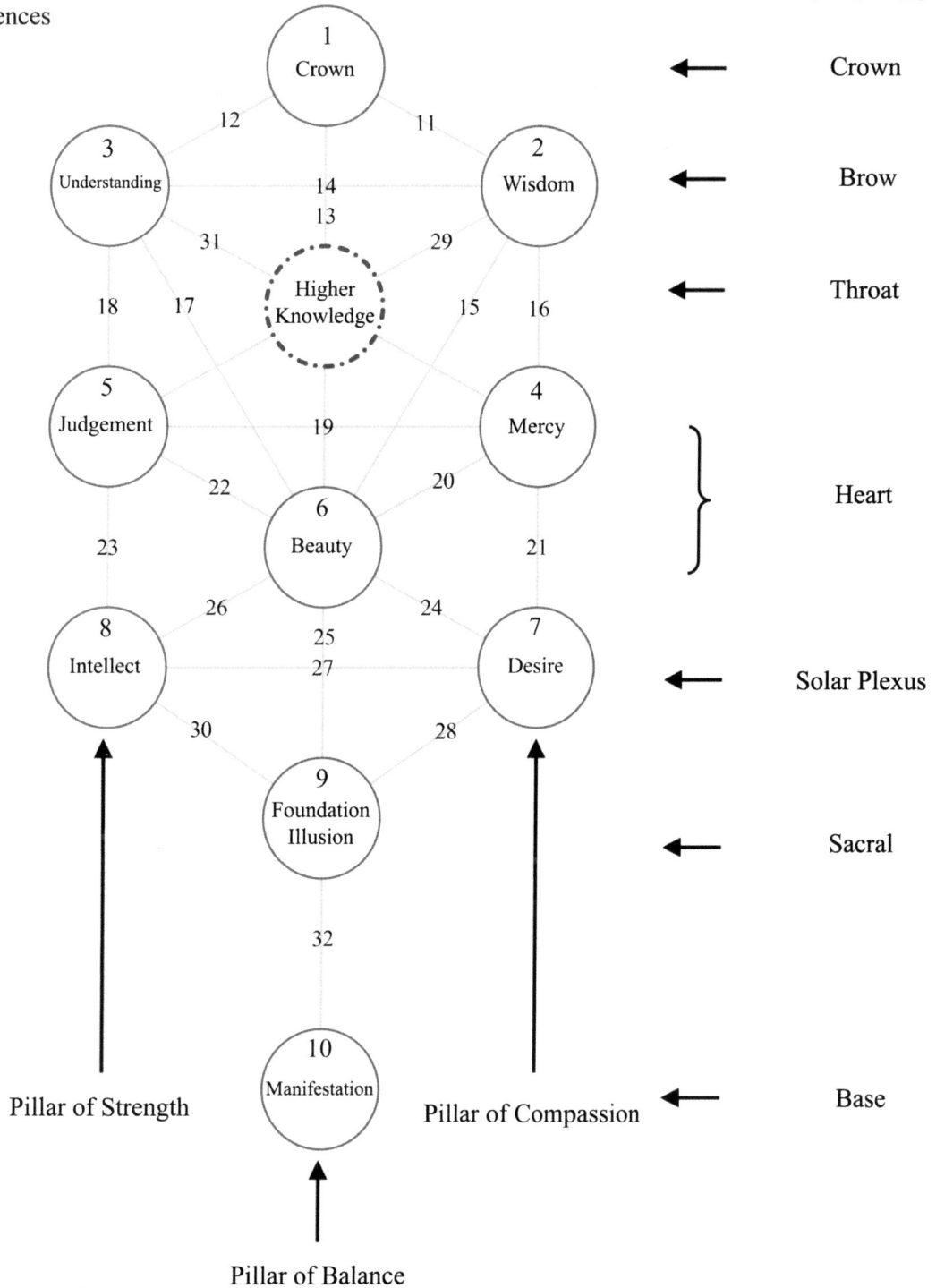

1 Crown	← Crown
12 11	
3 Understanding 14 2 Wisdom	← Brow
13	
31 Higher Knowledge 29	← Throat
18 17 15 16	
5 Judgement 19 4 Mercy	
22 20	Heart
6 Beauty 21	
23 26 25 24	
8 Intellect 27 7 Desire	← Solar Plexus
30 28	
9 Foundation Illusion	← Sacral
32	
10 Manifestation	← Base

Pillar of Strength

Pillar of Compassion

Pillar of Balance

Chakra is a Sanskrit word translating as a wheel or disc. Each one is a force of energy centred on the spinal column rising from the base of the spine to the top of the head. Rotating vortices of subtle matter they are focal points for the reception and transmission of energies. There are seven major chakras, six within the physical body, the seventh positioned just above the crown at the top of the head.

They are aspects of consciousness interacting with the physical body through two major vehicles, the endocrine system and the nervous system, each one correlating with seven endocrine glands, and an equal number of nerve plexuses. All senses, all perceptions, all states of awareness, every experience, can be categorised by the energies represented in these centres.

Thus, the chakras represent not only particular areas of the physical body, but also aspects of consciousness. Good health, emotional stability, mental clarity and spiritual wellbeing are achieved by bringing all these energies into balance.

The seven chakras are also said to reflect how the unified consciousness of man (the soul), is divided to manage different aspects of earthly life. They are placed at varying levels of spiritual subtlety, with the crown, at the top, being concerned with pure consciousness, and the base, at the bottom, connected to matter; fractured or dual consciousness.

Kabbalah meaning 'receiving', as represented in symbolic form by the Tree of Life, may be considered a map of consciousness, a blueprint of the universe, illustrating a path to spiritual illumination. A divine system of universal wisdom relating to man and his place in the cosmos it is a model for his ultimate potential, a way of understanding every aspect of his multi-dimensional nature.

It may be taught and learnt intellectually but its essence, its Truth lies in direct experience. Through contemplating and meditating upon the ten spheres (plus the one hidden sphere – Daath) and their 22 linking paths (each associated with the 22 letters of the Hebrew alphabet and the 22 major arcana in traditional tarot), a deep understanding of the essence of creation and the dynamic interplay of energies within the entirety of existence is delivered.

Keywords shown on each sphere along with the corresponding tarot archetypes provide simple avenues of exploration on which understanding gained from 'vision' and 'seed thought' may be expanded. The sphere of 'Daath', the hidden sphere, (displayed as 'Higher Knowledge' and 'Becoming', in the preceding diagrams) I believe to be of particular relevance in understanding the creative forces at play within these works of art.

Daath is a gateway. It is a space, a Great Void, which holds within it the entirety of existence. In the kabbalistic Tree of Life it is the sphere of Higher Knowledge, of inner knowing where nothing is taught yet everything is known. It is without definitive paths leading to the remaining ten spheres and yet it is in intimate relationship with all, including that of the highest sphere, the Divine Light of Emanation. The ways of this mysterious sphere are hidden and become visible only with the light of inner understanding. As such it may emerge, quite spontaneously, during exploration of any sphere ultimately leading to descent into and communion with the Abyss.

Associated with the throat in the eastern chakra system and the Vesica Piscis in Sacred Geometry, it is clearly a pathway to communion and an instigator of creativity, the supreme expression of which is the creation of life itself in its many and varied forms. Daath is a doorway to anywhere and anything but, in order to partake of the rich nectar held at its core, the personality must take a giant leap into the great unknown. It must surrender every idea, every notion, and every belief of which it perceives itself to be, and embrace the darkness of its own nature; the antithesis of all that is safe and all that is known.

However this darkness is the most trusted and safest place any personality could hope to encounter where surrender is the most natural, and indeed is the only response to its benevolent presence; it is a space *'where I may disappear and not even know I had gone'*. Its true nature is divine; Divine Darkness. It holds everything yet is nothing, a space of infinite stillness, infinite patience, infinite possibilities, infinite darkness that is absolute perfection. Yet this world is only arrived at through apparent chaos, destruction and death from the perspective of the ego self. There has to be an absolute let go where there is no ego, no self not even a 'higher self' or soul. There is nothing, absolutely nothing related to identity in any form.

And it is in this absolute nothingness that Truth may be realised. In unconditionally embracing the dark, in allowing its mystic essence to enfold, absorb and permeate every aspect of being, dark is transformed. As the self gives in to its embrace, dissolving completely, it becomes the very essence of dark, and with this immersion the light spontaneously arises from within. The infinite light of Daath can only be realised through total embracing of its dark. In supreme absorption, in consummate blackness, the light emerges triumphant.

Divine darkness is a receptive state. There is nothing to fix and nothing to impart, all is absolute perfection and all is known; all is dark and all is light. But the key lies in total surrender. Chaos, death, destruction and disease must be embraced with the highest reward being existential awareness from which anything is possible. In release and acceptance of all, moment by moment, there is nothing for the personality to 'do' but to receive, welcome and appreciate life. Simply receive. And in this receiving there is so much it is able to give.

Daath is Divine Darkness; a profound condition where dynamic stillness is charged with infinite potential, where all forms and identities are broken apart to be reformed in accordance with Divine Will. The womb of creation is all-inclusive whilst in essence being no thing. It is without doubt the most creative force in the entire universe. Its intimate connection with Divine Will cannot be disputed; the book of Genesis clearly describes the part played by both 'void' and 'darkness' in creation of heaven and earth:

"And the earth was without form, and void;
and darkness was upon the face of the deep."
Genesis 1:2

The next verse continues with the outpouring of light as an expression of the Will of God, also alluding to the association of sound, the voice and the throat chakra as playing essential parts in the unfolding of this Divine Plan for creation:

"And God *said*, Let there be light;
And there was light"
Genesis 1:3

We have only to observe the cycles within our own world to find natural order in decay and renewal; changing of seasons, ebb and flow of tides, night and day, life and death, each one of these bears testament to the powerful creative forces at play even at this physical level of reality. The evolution of consciousness, through personality, soul and beyond is no less subject to natural order than is our physical world. Soul integration, group initiation, every plane of existence from the smallest atom to the highest vibrations of light are subject to this same universal order of divine purpose; there are no exceptions. Alignment with this cosmic ordering, through the service of surrender, enables the individual to evolve into ever more refined vibrations of light, the ultimate reward being complete dissolution of the self into One Limitless Light.

Sacred Geometry

The construction of geometric shapes is simply geometry and as such holds little meaning, other than aesthetic, when being considered as a medium for contemplating realities; however when geometric principles are applied to levels of consciousness then simple geometry becomes sacred; Sacred Geometry.

What follows is a concise introduction beginning with a single circle evolving through seed, flower and fruit to create the five platonic solids: cube, tetrahedron, octahedron, icosahedron and dodecahedron. The elements contained within each of these structures sowed the seeds of inspiration for all cards within the 'Light' set. Generating these geometries requires three elementary implements – compass, straight edge and pencil. Starting with a compass we have a 'point' from which the creation process may begin. This bears a striking resemblance to the 'point of light' featured in the 'Creation' story earlier.

Taking our 'point' and a fixed radius a circle is drawn. This single circle creates the cause for the establishment of all reality from the highest vibrations of light, the simple circle, to the complexities of dense physical matter experienced within this earthly environment; as represented by the Fruit of Life. Nature in its infinite understanding grows and evolves through sacred geometric principle. Likewise sacred temples, churches etc throughout civilisation have as their source element the same inherent structure. The following diagrams illustrate the evolution of this process.

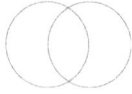
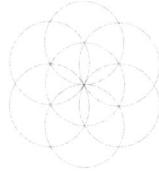
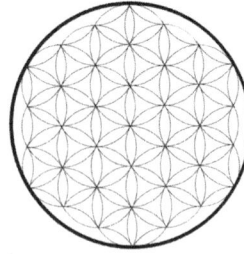
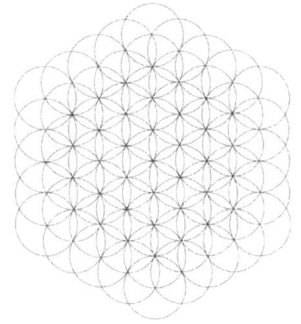

Circle   Vesica Piscis   Seed of Life   Flower of Life   Fruit of Life

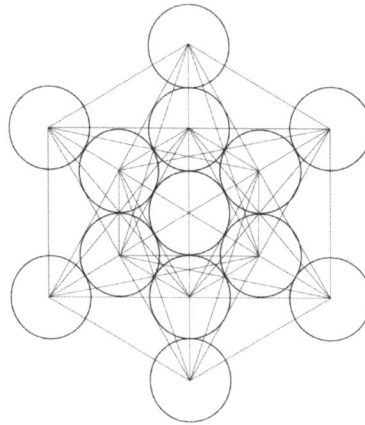

Metatron's Cube

ALL FIVE PLATONIC SOLIDS ARE EXTRACTED FROM THIS GEOMETRY

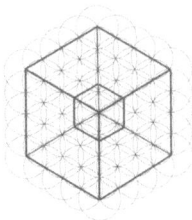

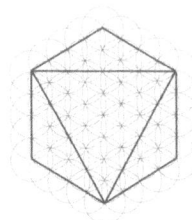
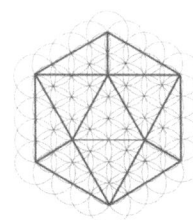
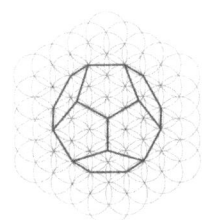

Cube   Star Tetrahedron   Octahedron   Icosahedron   Dodecahedron

Each solid is a level of consciousness and embodies certain qualities related to the evolution of matter into spirit, one of which is the five elements experienced within our natural environment.

Cube – Earth

Associated with the physical body and matter, the cube is most closely related to our experience of life within the confines of our comfort zone; the 'box' through which we view and create our reality. It is an unstable solid and requires something external to itself to support it; not unlike the personality when it lives according to fear based perceptions.

Tetra/Star Tetrahedron – Fire

This is the 'fire' of spirit or the higher mind. The star tetrahedron and the cube are 'duals' of each other - when turned on its side the star tetrahedron is in fact a cube. Being a stable solid, it is a powerful medium for stabilising the cube **from the inside** and offers equal opportunity for the personality to move beyond and transcend the limitations of the box. Incorporating upward and downward pointing tetrahedrons emphasising spirit and matter respectively, it also offers an expedient method for merging the personality with the soul.

Octahedron - Air

Another stable solid, the octahedron portrays the mental body and the lower mind. Although not directly connected with any other solid, it is nevertheless in intimate relationship with both the cube and star tetrahedron through the process of stellation (each face is extended from the centre to form a star shape); a stellated cube is an octahedron. In terms of personality integration control of the lower mind is of paramount importance. The octahedron holds within it both the previous geometries so is an effective method in cultivating awareness of the limitations of the cube whilst at the same supporting the unison offered by the star tetrahedron.

Icosahedron – Water

The emotional/astral bodies as well as the water element are represented by the icosahedron, another stable solid. Comprising 20 triangles, it offers substantial resolution for mastering the emotional/astral body, the most unstable of the subtle bodies. Feminine in nature, being almost spherical in shape, the icosa achieves harmony through the integrative nature of this triangular force held at its core.

Dodecahedron – Ether

The most unstable of all the solids the dodecahedron has as its quality the element of ether or prana (breath). The ethereal nature of this element, together with its instability, gives some indication of the level of consciousness required to achieve personality integration. Its dual is another feminine shape, the icosahedron, which acts as a stabilising and balancing agent, their intimate fusion establishing a stable dodeca harmonised from within.

In summary, the cube and star tetrahedron are masculine and duals, the icosahedron and dodecahedron are duals and feminine. The octahedron stands alone and is the divine child related to the masculine by stellation using control and the feminine by surrender.

Vesica Piscis

This is the geometric symbol for 'light'. These two interlocking circles represent divine communion; the true art of communication. In order for energy to flow between two aspects, two human beings, animal and human, spirit and matter etc. there must be an environment of receiving; a space **must** be created to allow free creative expression.

All too often, particularly in the case of human interactions, both parties either speak at once or interrupt each other whilst in full flow. As a result neither feels they have been heard. No surprise really for no-one has been listening; sincerely listening. The art of communion lies once more in surrender, each person has to 'get out of the way' and listen with the heart; this creates an interval, followed by expansion wherein understanding may flow in equal measure between each one.

"For creation to occur there must be a contraction, a concentration of energy to a single point followed by an expansion, an emanation into the space thus created."

This quote is taken from the 'Creation Story', its resonance echoing throughout the pages of this book particularly within the sphere of 'Daath' and repeating in ever increasing circles with the action of 'surrender'. Why should the art of communication be any different? Quite simply, it isn't, it's exactly the same process. Contraction, void, expansion; this is the Vesica Piscis, the divine *art* of communion.

Seed of Life

Seven concentric circles aligning seven chakras, seven rays, seven days of the week etc. are all displayed in non linear form naturally disclosing how the energy of each one flows and interacts as one perfected whole. This geometry holds within it the seed of all creation expanding through ever increasing rounds of concentric circles to produce the flower and ultimately the fruit of life. Nature follows the same divine order with seed containing the organic matrix for flower and fruit returning through death to release once more the seed. Each not only contains the other but **is** the other with natural evolution and perpetuation of the species assured. Our physical body is of the same order with each cell replicating the complex perfection of the human form. Sacred Geometry is indeed a blueprint for the entire universe.

Sphere

Stellated Dodecahedron

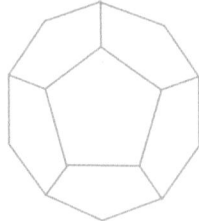

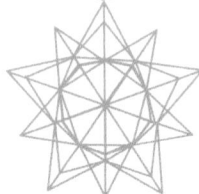

Dodecahedron

Stellated Icosaahedron

Icosahedron

Octahedron

Star Tetrahedron

Cube

Tetrahedron

Platonic Solids in Proportion to Consciousness

Graphic copyright: Barbara Rose, Ronald Holt ©2009.

Art of Synthesis

The *art* of Visions of Reality lies in its synthesising capabilities. Each tradition when contemplated from a holistic perspective in relation to its peer is found to amplify the inherent interrelationship between, not only the systems, but the fabric of life itself. Energy interplays between apparently separate ingredients are seen to enhance rather than detract from this essential wholeness. Marrying the insights gained from the visions' reflections with cohesive structures presented below carries potential for the highest level of soul integration to be realised.

Platonic Solids and the Chakras

First of all let it be said that every platonic solid may be found at each chakra emphasising the inclusive effect this may have on the discerning researcher of Truth. The following insights are derived from matching the elemental qualities of the solids with corresponding elements within the eastern chakra system; the rationale behind each placement being explained within each chakra.

Base - Earth

Concerned with basic survival and all that is related to physical existence, the base chakra naturally aligns to all fear-based perceptions including those connected to life in the 'box'. Placement of the cube at this position brings an unstable solid to a region that already has as its foundation potential instability. However, penetrating deeper into the secrets of the cube, there are very tangible and clear boundaries, qualities essential for transmuting fear-based perceptions into a balanced stable personality. The star tetrahedron dual, as mentioned above, is a means by which the cube may be stabilised **from within;** refinement of the personality being perpetual submission and blending of all perceived dualities within and without.

In addition it is wise to remember the cube from which all platonic solids are derived; metatron's cube. When viewed from this standpoint, it becomes evident that the ultimate level of spiritual inclusion may be realised when this inner journey is undertaken with humility and acceptance; grounding this in matter being of paramount importance.

Heart - Air

The air element together with its affiliation to the lower mind may seem at first glance an unusual bedfellow for the heart chakra. Surely the heart and love are an antithesis of mind, particularly intellectual mind? The heart however is a gateway to the infinite, to self realisation; it is the point of contact between body and soul, allowing passage to both spiritual and material worlds. When the lower mind resides in the heart, it succumbs to the all embracing wisdom of the heart; this thinking from the heart gives the highest aspect of love that holds neither emotion nor thought. Simplicity, purity of heart and intention along with infinite understanding are cornerstones of this placement; the child-like integrative nature and stability of the octahedron being obvious candidate for the position.

However, when the heart chakra is viewed within the Tree of Life, it can be seen to comprise not one but three spheres, their characters being Judgement, Mercy and Beauty with the octahedron (Freedom), dodecahedron (Devotion) and spiral (Trust) being the corresponding 'visions'. The dodecahedron is bliss and although a much expanded level of awareness it is nevertheless unstable. Placement at the heart as a stand alone solid without the broader understanding gained through the Tree of Life creates an expansion of love energy lacking in wisdom. Added to this, the element attuned to the dodeca is ether, a nebulous quality existing beyond the realms of the five physical senses, more suited to the vibration of sound and the throat.

The spiral is the energetic principle arising naturally through peaceful surrender in unison with the heart through the simple medium of trust. The word 'trust' in itself implies a total let-go, unconditional acceptance of all that is without judgement or agenda. It is the spiral that enables transition from one level of consciousness to another, from the micro to the macrocosm; it is the spiral of transcendence and the medium by which God realisation may be actualised.

Centres of Creativity – Sacral (Water), Throat (Ether) and Brow

Traditionally the sacral and throat chakras are known as the centres of creativity where one, the sacral, determines physical creation, sexuality, relationships etc. and the other, the throat, as the higher octave denotes creative expression in the form of sound, art, channelling etc. Both centres may be vehicles for the personality or for divine expression depending on the degree of resonance and harmony achieved through personality integration.

A third creative chakra vibrates at a higher octave to the other two and that is the brow; the centre of creative thought. When the energy between these three centres is flowing in perfect harmony, the creative forces of the universe, by conscious intent (brow) find creative expression (throat) in the form of harmonious relationships and pro-creative activity (sacral). The interactions between these three chakras are predominantly, however, an inner process where the healing of childhood/past life conditioning results in clarity of mind/vision, freedom of expression and harmonious relationships.

The platonic solids associated with these energy centres are icosahedron (sacral), dodecahedron (throat) and the stellated icosahedron (brow). These have been shown to have an intimate affinity with each other; the icosa and dodeca being duals and the stellated icosa being direct expansion of the icosa through cultivation of single pointed focal awareness. Placement of the icosa at the sacral chakra is self evident as its inherent rapport with the waters of life provides its obvious justification, but what of the dodeca and its kinship to bliss? How may bliss be stable at the throat yet not in the heart?

The answer lies in the intricate interplay of energies between all three geometries. Stability at the lowest creative centre, the sacral, enables natural expansion of the throat (the dodeca is stabilised from within by the icosa) in a balanced and harmonious way. The stellated icosa at the brow culminates in clear-seeing, profound awareness, stimulating further natural expansion of the throat. When the throat is purified, holding no blocks to expression, the energy may flow freely between the heart and brow. The mind is still, the heart is all encompassing wisdom in action, the throat is pure and open; this is bliss, the stable dodeca.

Solar Plexus (Fire), Throat and Brow

These three chakras are similarly linked; the endocrine glands associated with each one showing physiological interactions through these regions within the framework of the physical body. Pranic energy is absorbed through the spleen (solar plexus) and distributed throughout the physical body by thyroxin, the hormone secreted by the thyroid gland (throat); the anterior pituitary gland (brow) regulates the function of the thyroid which also plays a large part in regulating metabolism and, as a consequence, the digestion process (solar plexus).

The solar plexus is the seat of the ego self, the locus for our "gut feelings", and the highest chakra directly connected to the personality. It is the centre of the will and the spirit bridge between heaven and earth where human will is eventually transformed into divine will. The thyroid (means 'door') gland, as an activity within the throat chakra, balances brain function (brow), and is the highest chakra where the personality finds expression. Its level of balance determines whether emotions are in control or there is stillness of mind. Freedom of movement within and between each of these energy centres is of paramount importance to ensure physical well-being, emotional stability and peace of mind, where the personality may ultimately evolve into a vehicle whose primary task is to be of service to the soul. The solar plexus thus radiates divine will, the throat is creative expression of divine purpose and the brow is a channel for divine intent.

Throat and brow having already been considered, the only remaining chakra to be examined within this section is the solar plexus, represented by the star tetrahedron and the fire element. As already stated, this is the centre of will, the centre of the ego self, the final battleground of the personality; no wonder its core substance is fire! The fires of passion are the burning ground for the soul and as such a powerful symbol is required to assimilate the energies being transformed. The star tetrahedron is more than a match for this task holding within it the very essence of spirit and matter. Integration is eventually assured; the will of the personality succumbs to that of the divine gradually evolving into a perfected vessel for soul purpose.

Sacral, Solar Plexus, Throat and Brow - Synthesis

Understandings gained from considering the elemental aspects to these four chakras may now be measured against the Tree of Life diagram. Beginning at the sacral we find a single sphere, the sphere of Illusion, personified by the 'vision' Arcturus revealing an intricate structure containing both seed and flower of life; not the icosahedron as mapped out above. The solar plexus brings in two spheres, Intellect and Desire, represented by Apocalypse and Genesis, geometric forms being the star tetrahedron and icosahedron respectively. At the throat (Higher Knowledge) lies, not the dodecahedron, but the Vesica Piscis showing two complete seeds with interlocking Tree of Life diagrams; the vision is 'Becoming'. Finally the brow reveals a further two spheres Wisdom and Understanding, being Divine Darkness and Divine Inspiration respectively; the geometry on each being the Seed of Life with the Tree of Life superimposed. No sign of the stellated icosahedron as mentioned in the chakra interpretations.

At first glance this could completely negate the rationale for chakra/geometry/tree alignment. However when the bigger picture is reflected upon a tapestry of holistic consistency emerges. The sacral, throat and brow each have as their component parts the Seed of Life; when two spheres at the brow are joined together they become the Vesica Piscis as revealed in the 'Becoming' drawing. Arcturus at the sacral is a portal, the seed of creation, leading inwards through unending spirals to reveal the flower of life; its full potential being realised as the crowning fruit of life. Consistent links with the centres of creativity is maintained. Furthermore I believe these centres of creativity to be gateways to higher dimensions; the platonic solids being effective on one level with the 'seeds' providing access to another.

Apparent misplacement of icosa and dodecahedron may now be understood from a wider perspective. Tree of Life analysis reveals both the icosa and star tetrahedron to be positioned at the solar plexus. The elements concerned are water and fire respectively; harmonising of these two elements is fundamental to personality integration. Contemplations of the visions show each sphere to be represented by not one but two aspects of the same drawing; Apocalypse Fire/Water and Genesis Inception/Manifestation; further emphasising the unifying effect these elements have when brought into balance. The solar plexus spheres of Intellect and Desire when considered as a triangular force with that of Illusion, at the sacral centre, offer the highest potential to transcend all emotional baggage.

Similarly the dodeca, 'Devotion', position as one of the spheres within the heart centre has a wider interpretation. This drawing has not one but three aspects, Compassion, Clarity and Unity, and has a synthesising effect on many vibrations. On a basic level it achieves integrative balance as part of the triangular force at the heart; refinement of the personality seeing the emergence of compassion and clarity of mind. With this emergence the three aspects of the dodeca move to a higher vibration activating more spheres on the Tree of Life. This higher triad encompasses the spheres Mercy (Devotion-dodeca) and Judgement (Octa-Freedom) at the heart centre, and Higher Knowledge (Vesica Piscis-Becoming) at the throat

Crown

This is the Godhead, the Crowning Glory, Buddha Mind and the Thousand Petalled Lotus of eastern spiritual traditions. The aspiration of every spiritual seeker is to reach this point of illumination and many lifetimes have been spent in furtherance of this aim. Is it a worthwhile goal or does its pursuit take the seeker deeper into the realm of illusion? Maybe Sacred Geometry will provide a clue.

Sitting at this position on the Tree of Life is the 'Gnosis' drawing depicting the fruit of life, whilst the crown chakra is shown to display the stellated dodecahedron, the Christ Consciousness grid. Each of these geometries holds within it the entire fabric of existence and provides valuable keys to the question posed above. Reviewing all our understanding gained from contemplating these systems have shown that every solid is derived from the fruit of life; Metatron's cube. And which solid lies at the base chakra as well as the 'lowest' sphere of the tree? The cube!

All our lives are spent searching for something which we perceive to be beyond/above/outside of where we are when the answer lays literally beneath our nose. We already are that which we seek. The Gnosis vision offers some guidance with respect to this wisdom and has three qualities reflecting the primary aspects of divinity; Love (Purity), Mind (Intelligence) and Will (Tranquillity). The Greek word 'Gnosis' refers to knowledge acquired through experience. It is conscious and experiential and directly related to moment by moment existence. Therein lays the answer to man's spiritual quest for enlightenment. Be still, and know that you are God.

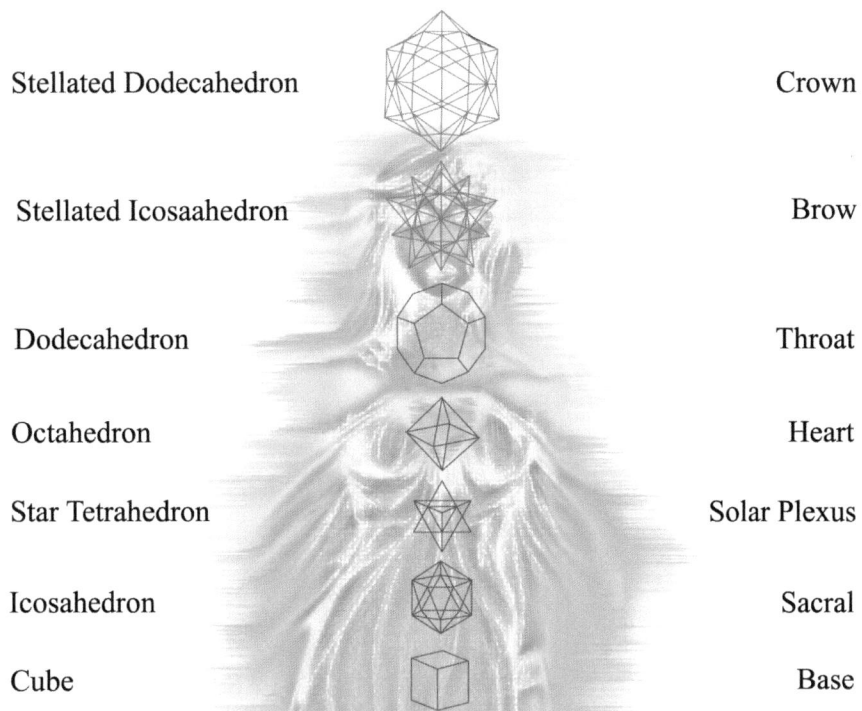

Stellated Dodecahedron		Crown
Stellated Icosaahedron		Brow
Dodecahedron		Throat
Octahedron		Heart
Star Tetrahedron		Solar Plexus
Icosahedron		Sacral
Cube		Base

Platonic Solids and Related Chakras

Conclusion

Taking all these aspects into consideration, it can be seen nothing is straightforward or black and white when determining affinities between solids, chakras and the inner workings of the Tree of Life. As already mentioned, every solid may be found at every chakra with each aspect being likened to a multi-faceted diamond; the preceding analysis taking into consideration a fraction of the information contained within these holistic structures. It is only through reflection that understanding may arise naturally from within; this is inner knowing. Intellectual argument cannot provide adequate testament to ultimate Truth particularly when measured against reflective avenues of exploration.

Contemplation of these systems and indeed of life itself takes me deeper and deeper into the subtleties of all to reveal delicate gossamer threads of light, weaving an intricate web of interrelations where the intricacies of each system is shown to have intimate affinity with all. No man is an island and by the same association neither is a system, a chakra, a solid or a sphere each one being a window of opportunity, a doorway, through which the world may be viewed and experienced from a perspective of holistic awareness.

As human beings we are conduits through which spiritual and earthly realms may unite. We are bridges between levels of existence where planetary and cosmic worlds are brought into alignment and it is the highest purpose of each and everyone of us to evolve our level of conscious awareness, our alignment with Great Spirit, so the need for these bridges becomes redundant; no heaven, no earth, no bridge, no system; all boundaries and separation having dissolved into existential union with All That Is.

Each platonic solid is found at every chakra centred on the spinal column and may be seen as spiralling vortices of energy extending to the front and rear of the physical body.

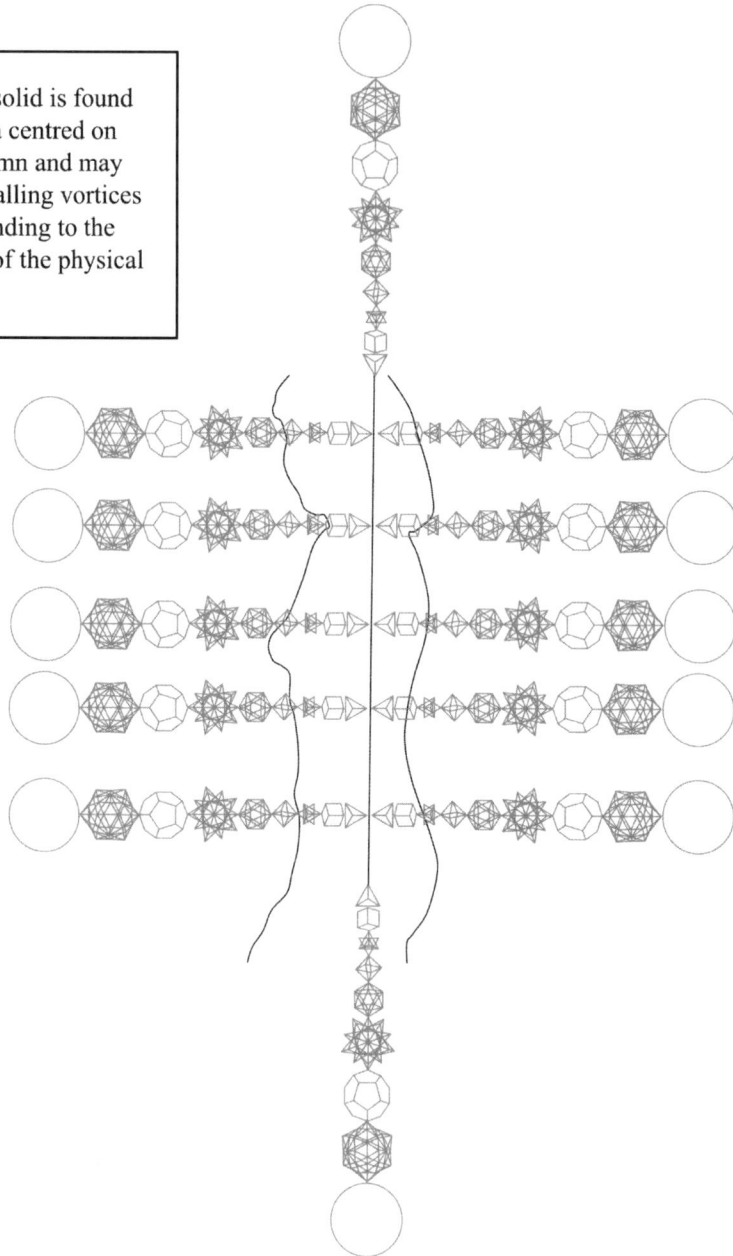

Graphic copyright Barbara Rose, Ronald Holt ©2009

Beyond
all Systems

"Be Still and Know that I am God"

Psalm 48:10

Three visions, A Point of Light, Illumination, A Walk in the Park, lie beyond 'the system' and as such do not form relationships with either the sets or paths within the Tree of Life. The seed thought connected with each one is paradoxically simple and obscure requiring more space and time to reveal the treasure held within its core; contemplation and meditation are the suggested means by which this may be achieved. The following insights gained from the inspiration behind each image may be of some assistance and offer signposts on your journey.

A Point of Light

This relates to the creation story at the beginning of the book. The opening poem 'The Great Invocation' may also give further clues to assist. Contemplating the point of origin of all creation, including that of 'Daath', provides valuable insight into the journey we must make to affect our return.

Illumination

This drawing was inspired through contemplation of the planet Neptune and contains vast potential for pushing beyond the boundaries of this physical existence. It is the planet of dreams, visions, illusion and addiction. Its subtle nature indicating the highest spiritual potential, of which this planet reigns supreme, may only be attained through embracing the darkness of one's own being. The seed thought reflects this subtlety and comes in the form of a Zen koan needing an enquiring mind to penetrate the secrets of the deep Truth held at its centre. Only you can do this.

A Walk in the Park

The simplicity, magic and ordinariness of everyday life inspired release of this vision. It is the enlightened human who has integrated his personality with his soul and walks upon this earth in full eminence of his authentic nature. The seed thought provides a clue as to the journey he has undertaken to reach this point of evolution.

Additional Guidance

Truth is the essence behind each of these Visions. They are the 'enlightened human', the integrated personality whose 'raison d'être' is to be of service to the soul. It is suggested they be contemplated as a triad with each 'Vision' and 'seed thought' being a unified expression of the three primary Rays of God – Will and Power (A Point of Light), Love-Wisdom (Illumination) and Active Intelligence (A Walk in the Park).

Your guidance, if any, is to surrender your intellectual understanding, contemplate each one and allow the Truth of your own being to awaken from within. Most importantly, live your life in accordance with that Truth. Be still, and know that you are God. Namaste...

A Point of Light

A turn of the spiral sees dark take new form...

Illumination

…? the sound of the sea as it touches the sky?

A Walk in the Park

All that you are master become
Master of all, master of none

Surrender

"When I turn within to explore the space from which my heart takes form. I find there is no form, there is no heart. There is simply vast empty space, a void that holds the entirety of my existence, all existence. It is a giant, joyful wave that carries me from one moment to the next embracing all in its path. All my wants, desires, needs, feelings, thoughts dissolve into this vast ocean of consummate wholeness.

And there is smiling inside. I am not even sure whether it is I who is smiling; it seems to arise quite spontaneously for no apparent reason. Others have noticed and observe 'you look like the cat that got the cream'. Well, I am the cat who got the cream but there is no cream; nothing external gives rise to this incredible joy that bubbles silently within...

...And in a moment of profound, silent awareness a question is born, a thought-form cast from within the great void upon the mirror of my mind: 'Why am I here?' It hangs suspended, like a water droplet, apparently frozen in time, seeking substance until time itself releases it once more unto the void. For a while it rests within the great ocean of infinite possibilities until the next wave throws it once more onto the surface of my mind, 'Why am I here?' Lazy tendrils of enquiry seek dark recess in my concrete mind for an answer, even finding some resolution, once again I let go, the droplet having no more substance is again released; all is still...

...another thought, larger and more substantial than before, arises. It holds within it a story, a story of creation: "Great Spirit, whilst resting in absolute totality of being, as pure awareness, gave birth to a thought: 'how would it be if I did not know myself?' In that moment, with the issue of this simple thought, the world of duality, the world as we know it, was born..."

Now I had two thought bubbles to ponder upon. They hung together in suspended animation as if the pause button had been pressed on my mind; two tiny droplets held within an even greater bubble of awareness. Before long I realised one held resolution for the other. In unison they merged to become far more than the sum of their two parts. They were yin and yang, divine mother and divine father, enjoining in sacred union that the blessed child of infinite understanding be born to illuminate the far reaches of my mind and the immeasurable depths of my heart...

...I am here to experience duality and the deeper my experience, the more I sink into this realm of separation, the closer I am to the original question posed by Great Spirit. I am in immanent proximity to that first moment of creation. Experience and question unite and consciously I participate in duality, allowing myself to sink deeper and deeper into form without becoming identified with it; a wondrous alchemical transformation takes place. In the clear light of my illuminate mind, in the infinite bounds of my heart, I am Great Spirit experiencing duality through me. This is why I am here. It really is that simple."

In living this understanding, recognition of two keywords are paramount, 'experiencing' and 'identification'. When I am 'the wave', the continuous wave of infinite possibilities, I am one with Great Spirit; each moment in my life is experiencing, there is no self and no other, no union and no separation, all is just as it is: very simple and very ordinary. However, if I identify with any of these things: myself, another, an experience, memory, need, desire, physical body, even union with Great Spirit then I am back in the world of duality. I become separate and in that moment pain in my heart ensues; isolation, loneliness, physical pain, all my wants and needs become driving forces in my life.

There is a subtle veil which transmutes one way of being into the other: it is quite simply, awareness; pure awareness. The shift in consciousness from one way of being to another is an inner process where the fire of awareness burns through destructive forces of divisive thought. This all consuming fire has one or two very trusted friends; courage and surrender. Without their participation, awareness may as well return to its slumbers and allow the fires of passion to rule the roost. In other words unless awareness is acted upon, it serves no purpose. The journey continues.

"Through space and time have I travelled to see past and future merge into this present moment, where absolute clarity of mind is the all embracing wisdom of my heart; the notion of 'other' being simply thought to transform. I see how many parts compose the labyrinth that is my small self, how separate and isolate they are in their multiplicity, and how, within a single moment of awareness, they may dissolve into one great river of joyous simplicity; the Self. Cultivating awareness of this 'Self' enables soul purpose to be made visible and when I surrender, when I step aside, all barriers dissolve and in the stillness of each moment it flows, as a steady stream, to enrich the content of my days with reverent appreciation.

As threads of light weave their way through the tapestry that is my life, an image slowly begins to take form... shimmering in vibrant, radiant, diamond clear light, against the background of my days... it is the totality of all my experiences: meetings and partings, sorrow and joy, happiness and despair, fear and love... All I have ever known in countless existences since beginning of time... it carries the heartbeat of the universe, one glorious note to echo the entirety of existence; the vibration of absolute perfection... AUM"

Extracts from an article: Why am I here? A Journey through Space and Time by Barbara Rose ©2008

Glossary

Flower of Life Research Organisation created to disseminate the teachings of the merkaba, sacred geometry, (as originally presented by Drunvalo Melchizedek) as well as the opening of the heart. They also provide methods to integrate the left brain (mind) and the right brain (heart/feeling/intuition) into a fluid understanding of the cosmos that is not only intellectually understood but also tangibly experienced. These teachings help inspire individuals to remember who they really are and to find the courage to expand beyond their limited views of themselves.

Fractal is "a rough or fragmented geometric shape that can be split into parts, each of which is (at least approximately) a reduced-size copy of the whole". Natural objects that are approximated by fractals include clouds, mountain ranges, lightning bolts, coastlines, snowflakes, various vegetables (cauliflower and broccoli), and animal coloration patterns.

http://en.wikipedia.org/w/index.php?title=Fractal&oldid=337402491

Inner Knowing is a doorway to the infinite. It is direct experiential knowledge derived through the intuition rather than intellectual reasoning. Generating understanding, through meditation or contemplation, is thinking from the heart, a marriage of heart and mind.

Mandala "a Sanskrit word meaning 'essence' or 'containing' may also be a term for any geometric pattern that represents the cosmos." It is a microcosm of the universe and used extensively in Buddhist meditation practices to focus the mind on the sacred holy ground of the Buddha. 'Visions of Reality' images may be viewed as sacred mandalas particularly those from the 'Light Set'. All sacred geometry is holographic and a representation of the cosmos.

http://en.wikipedia.org/w/index.php?title=Mandala&oldid=337334338

Mantra/Mantram "is a sound, syllable, word or group of words that are considered capable of creating transformation." The most well known is the sacred Om/Aum. Essentially 'thought forms' they may be used to create positive change and to manifest divinity within ordinary life. The 'seed thoughts' associated with the images and sets may be considered as mantras.

http://en.wikipedia.org/w/index.php?title=Mantra&oldid=336488524

Merkaba is a counter-rotating field of light generated from the spinning of specific geometric forms that simultaneously affect one's spirit and body. It is a vehicle that can aid mind, body and spirit to access and experience other planes of reality or potentials of life. A crystalline energy field, comprised of specific sacred geometries that align the mind, body, and heart together, it extends around the body for a distance of 55 feet and normally spins at close to the speed of light. However, for most of us, it has slowed down or stopped spinning entirely, due to a lack of attention and use. When this field is reactivated and spinning properly, it is called a Merkaba. A fully activated Merkaba looks just like the structure of a galaxy or a UFO.

©1999, 2000, 2001 Flower of Life Research LLC All Rights Reserved.

Namaste is "a Sanskrit word meaning quite simply 'I bow to you'. The word is derived from 'namas', meaning 'to bow', and 'te' meaning 'to you'. However there is a reverential meaning attached to it which is used most frequently within spiritual greeting, *I bow to you. The light within me honors the light within you'*, hands are held at the heart in prayer position as the greeting is sounded." It is this reverence that is intended within the context of this book.

http://en.wikipedia.org/w/index.php?title=Namaste&oldid=335074594

Seed Thought may be considered a modern expression of a mantra. (see above)

Seven Rays associated with this work are those based on the teachings of Alice A. Bailey. The seven may be categorised into three primary rays of aspect and four secondary rays of attribute; four are assigned to 'love' and three to 'will'. According to AAB each person has a soul ray, that remains the same through all incarnations, and a personality ray that changes with each life. Rays also correspond to Masters of the Wisdom, to planets, constellations, cycles, nations etc. It is a vast subject so, for simplicity, only the three primary rays are touched upon in this book.

http://en.wikipedia.org/w/index.php?title=Seven_rays&oldid=331899180

Visions of Reality - Resources

All visions featured in this book are available as prints, canvases or greeting cards. It is anticipated a full colour set of contemplation cards will be available in the near future. For more information please see website below. Additional direction amplifying the content of this book is also posted on the site together with information on talks, workshops and presentations etc.

Web: www.visionsofreality.co.uk
Email: mail4@visionsofreality.co.uk

Further Reading

Ancient Wisdom

The Emerald Tablets of Thoth the Atlantean: Doreal
The Heart of Wisdom: Thich Nhat Hanh
The Seven Rays of Life: Alice A. Bailey
The Labours of Hercules – An Astrological Interpretation: Alice A. Bailey
Stages of Meditation: H.H. the Dalai Lama

Chakras

Exploring Chakras – Awaken your untapped Energy: By Susan G. Shumsky
Chakras and their Archetypes – Uniting Energy Awareness and Spiritual Growth: Ambika Waters

Kabbalah

The Secret Doctrine of the Kabbalah: Leonara Leet
A Kabbalistic Universe: Z'ev ben Shimon Halevi
The Shining Paths: Dolores Ashcroft-Nowicki
The Complete Guide to the Kabbalah: Will Parfitt

Sacred Geometry

Flower of Life Research: www.floweroflife.org
Article: The Convergence of 2012 and the Sacred Geometry of Integration: Ronald Holt
http://floweroflife.org/rh-convergence2012.pdf
Article: The Spiral and the Holographic Matrix: Ronald Holt
http://floweroflife.org/holomatrix01.htm
Article: Meditation and the Art of Merging: Ronald Holt
http://floweroflife.org/medit01.htm
A Beginners Guide to Constructing the Universe – the Mathematical Archetypes of Nature, Art and Science: Michael S. Schneider
The Ancient Secret of the Flower of Life Vol 1 and Vol 2: Drunvalo Melchizedek
The Golden Section – Nature's Greatest Secret: Scott Olsen

Other

The Heindl Tarot – the Major Arcana: Rachel Pollack

About the Author

Barbara Rose is a researcher of Truth. Her inner journey began in earnest at the turn of the century when ill health forced a change in focus from the outer to the inner. Relinquishing her former profession as an Air Traffic Controller she set out on a journey of Self discovery choosing tai chi, homeopathy and meditation as mediums for inner expansion. Embarking on four long term courses in furtherance of that aim she emerged as a Homeopath and Infinite Tai Chi, and Meditation teacher some three years later. A far cry from air traffic control!

Tai chi, homeopathy, meditation, courses, workshops, retreats and personal development became foundations for her inner journey. In five short years she witnessed considerable transformation within her emotional body opening her heart to compassionate understanding. Ultimately this transformation led to total surrender and release of all identities she had spent the last five years creating!

Release and surrender will almost certainly culminate in communion with the abyss which if welcomed holds ultimate creative potential. "Empty and be filled" are wise words indeed and this was certainly true for Barbara; release of all identities ignited the creative spark leading to the production of her first drawing.

Guided by several spiritual teachers and healers, over many years, she now offers the wisdom of her experience, in service to others, facilitating ease of transformation through talks, workshops and contemplation groups. Her passion and vision is to see ultimate creative expression integrated into the daily lives of all.

"As I reflect upon my life I see my entire journey has led to this point. This work is pure joy to create and fills me with excitement at its potential."

She lives in Preston, UK with two cosmic cats and Jonty Sunbeam Spirit-Walker; a canine Sirian graced with radiant joy who decorates even the most dismal wintry days with sun kissed perfection.

Index

LaVergne, TN USA
24 May 2010
1800LVUK00002B